Swift

Programming

Handbook

A Realistic Guide for Building iOS Apps Efficiently

STEVEN S. BELLS

TABLE OF CONTENTS

Part I
Groundwork of Practical Swift Programming

Understanding Swift in a Real-World Context

Why Swift Remains the Go-To for iOS Development

Swift has positioned itself as the preferred programming language for iOS development due to its efficiency, clarity, and long-term maintainability. Unlike many languages that attempt to serve multiple domains equally, Swift was built with a deliberate focus on mobile development, particularly for Apple's platforms. It prioritizes structure, readability, and safety, which directly translates into fewer bugs, better user experience, and a smoother development process.

The language offers a balance between strict type safety and developer flexibility. This blend allows developers to catch potential errors during the coding stage, well before they escalate into runtime failures. Such early detection is crucial in mobile development, where app performance and reliability significantly impact user retention.

Moreover, Swift code compiles to highly optimized native binaries. This leads to faster app launch times, responsive interfaces, and efficient memory usage—qualities essential for mobile applications running on resource-constrained devices. In a market where milliseconds make a difference in user perception, Swift delivers where it matters.

The language is also supported by a growing community and an open development process. Swift's source code is available publicly, and proposals for language changes are reviewed with community input. This transparency keeps it modern and adaptable to real-world demands. For developers building iOS applications today, Swift is not just the official tool—it is the practical one.

Language Philosophy: Safety, Performance, Expressiveness

Swift was engineered around three guiding principles: safety, performance, and expressiveness. These are not marketing slogans but observable characteristics that shape how developers interact with the language daily.

Safety is perhaps Swift's most talked-about attribute. By design, Swift avoids entire classes of common programming errors. For example, the introduction of optionals forces developers to explicitly handle the absence of a value, rather than relying on implicit assumptions that often lead to crashes. This results in code that is more predictable, more testable, and easier to review. Type inference further enhances safety by ensuring that variables are used as intended, reducing misinterpretation and unintended behavior.

Performance is where Swift quietly outpaces its predecessor. It leverages a modern compiler infrastructure that generates highly optimized machine code. The language supports value types such as structs and enums that reduce the overhead of reference counting, which was a performance bottleneck in older codebases written in other languages. It also integrates tightly with low-level C and system libraries when needed, providing a path for developers to write high-performance routines without sacrificing safety or readability.

Expressiveness enables developers to write less code while achieving more. Swift's syntax encourages the use of powerful constructs such as higher-order functions, concise closures, and built-in generics. These features allow complex logic to be represented clearly and succinctly. Unlike verbose languages that require boilerplate, Swift promotes concise solutions that still maintain clarity and function. This expressiveness is not about writing clever one-liners—it's about producing logic that is maintainable and elegant over time.

Together, these three principles form a development experience that is intuitive, structured, and optimized for both human and machine understanding. Swift lets programmers think about logic and design, not memory leaks or unexpected type conversions.

The Evolving Swift Ecosystem

Swift is not static. It is a language that continues to grow in direct response to real-world development challenges. Each major release introduces features that improve productivity, encourage clean architectural patterns, and reduce boilerplate.

For example, the introduction of **concurrency features** in Swift 5.5 brought structured concurrency to the language in a way that's approachable and consistent. Tasks, async/await syntax, and actors significantly reduce the complexity of writing asynchronous code. These changes make concurrency not only safer but also easier to reason about, especially in applications with network calls, animations, or background data processing.

Another significant shift is the gradual rise of **SwiftUI** as a modern UI framework. While SwiftUI is not required to write applications, it represents a forward-looking approach to UI development where state drives behavior and layout. This complements Swift's language design by removing imperative complexity and aligning interface logic with the principles of composability and reusability.

The Swift Package Manager has also matured into a reliable tool for dependency management and modularization. It simplifies how developers share code, organize large projects, and adopt third-party libraries. Combined with advancements in tooling such as improved auto-completion, refactoring aids, and static analysis, Swift development has become more seamless than ever.

Importantly, Swift's cross-platform potential is slowly expanding. Although its primary usage remains within the Apple ecosystem, there are growing communities applying Swift on server-side projects and other platforms. This broadens Swift's utility and makes it a language worth learning even outside the iOS context.

In summary, Swift continues to reflect the realities of modern software engineering. Its evolution is shaped not by trends but by practical needs. From safer syntax to better tools, from mobile-first focus to cross-platform capabilities,

Swift is moving in a direction that prioritizes stability, clarity, and long-term code health.

Swift Essentials with Real-World Applications

Variables, Constants, and Optionals — Practical Use Cases

Understanding how to handle data in Swift begins with mastering variables, constants, and optionals. These are not abstract concepts but daily tools for managing state, enforcing logic, and handling uncertainty within software systems.

Variables and Constants: Choosing the Right Declaration

Swift uses `var` for variables and `let` for constants. The decision between the two has direct implications for code clarity and stability. Constants (`let`) signal immutability, and their use acts as a safeguard against accidental reassignment, especially in logic-heavy codebases. This is crucial in environments where unintended state changes can result in erratic app behavior.

In practical projects, constants are ideal for fixed configuration values—such as maximum character limits, URLs, or reusable styling properties. For example:

```
let maxLoginAttempts = 3
let apiEndpoint = "https://api.example.com/user"
```

Variables (`var`), on the other hand, should only be used when mutation is expected. A counter tracking screen views or a buffer holding real-time user input might require a mutable value:

```
var userInput = ""
```

```
var loginAttempts = 0
```

Being intentional about when to use `var` prevents unintended behavior and encourages better architecture.

Optionals: Writing Defensive Code

Optionals allow values to exist in either a filled or empty state. This is not just a language novelty—it's a way of making your code safer. Swift forces developers to explicitly account for the absence of values, preventing common crashes caused by null references.

For instance, when parsing user input or working with APIs that might not return data, optionals offer a structured way to handle these scenarios:

```
var userAge: Int? = Int("25") // might fail to convert
```

Using constructs like `if let`, `guard let`, and optional chaining lets developers safely interact with values that may or may not exist:

```
if let age = userAge {
    print("User is \(age) years old")
} else {
    print("Invalid age input")
}
```

This approach minimizes runtime surprises by pushing validation and verification to the point of use, where it belongs.

Control Flow and Functions That Scale

Control Flow: Clarity through Structured Logic

Swift's control flow statements—such as `if`, `switch`, `while`, and `for`—promote code that is readable and traceable. What sets Swift apart is its support for advanced control patterns, such as pattern matching within `switch` statements and support for labeled loops.

The `switch` structure in Swift supports value binding and ranges, which simplifies branching logic in decision-heavy codebases. For example:

let statusCode = 404

```
switch statusCode {
case 200:
    print("Success")
case 400...499:
    print("Client error")
case 500...599:
    print("Server error")
default:
    print("Unknown status")
}
```

This level of expressiveness allows developers to reduce deeply nested `if-else` trees, leading to cleaner logic.

Functions: Designing for Reuse and Scale

Functions in Swift can be written with parameters, return types, and default values, allowing for high levels of configurability. More importantly, Swift supports function overloading and parameter labels, making the intent behind a function call clearer.

```
func greet(name: String, isMorning: Bool = true) {
    if isMorning {
        print("Good morning, \(name)!")
    } else {
```

```
    print("Hello, \(name).")
  }
}
```

Well-structured functions help reduce repetition and isolate logic. This becomes especially important in production systems where small changes can affect wide portions of the codebase.

Additionally, Swift encourages developers to make use of function types and higher-order functions such as map, filter, and reduce, which are essential for modern data-driven development.

Closures, Enums, and Structs — Production-Level Patterns

Closures: Encapsulating Behavior

Closures are self-contained blocks of functionality that can be passed and used in code. They are commonly used for callbacks, asynchronous logic, and as building blocks for functional patterns.

```
let multiply = { (a: Int, b: Int) -> Int in
    return a * b
}
```

In applications, closures play a significant role in animation blocks, event handling, and network response processing. They allow developers to encapsulate logic that can be reused or executed at a later time, which is vital for modern interactive applications.

Swift's syntax makes closures concise while retaining clarity. When used properly, closures contribute to modularity and responsiveness without sacrificing readability.

Enums: Modeling Finite State with Precision

Enums in Swift are powerful tools for modeling clearly defined states. With support for associated values and methods, enums go far beyond simple integer representations.

```
enum LoginState {
    case idle
    case loading
    case success(userID: String)
    case failure(error: String)
}
```

Using enums in state management enables precise control over what values are valid under certain conditions. This helps enforce strict logic in network operations, form validation, and user navigation flows. Instead of scattering conditionals across the code, developers can manage state transitions in a centralized and descriptive way.

Structs: Value Semantics and Code Clarity

Structs are used extensively in Swift for creating lightweight, immutable types that benefit from value semantics. They are ideal for representing models, configurations, and data carriers that don't require shared reference behavior.

For instance:

```
struct User {
    let id: String
    var name: String
}
```

Since structs are copied when passed around, they reduce the likelihood of unintended side effects. This is particularly useful in environments where predictability and thread-safety are important.

Swift structs can also adopt protocols and contain methods, making them suitable even for moderately complex data representations. Their use promotes a cleaner separation between data and behavior, which improves testability and maintenance over time.

Working with Types and Protocols Effectively

Efficient Swift development requires a strong grasp of how types interact with one another and how abstraction can be structured for code reuse without sacrificing clarity. Swift offers a refined type system, sophisticated protocol capabilities, and powerful generic tools that allow developers to write cleaner, safer, and more scalable code. This section provides detailed insights into practical use cases of advanced types, protocol-oriented design, and generics.

Advanced Type Inference and Constraints

Understanding Type Inference

Swift employs type inference to reduce boilerplate while maintaining type safety. When a type is clear from context, the compiler infers it automatically. This improves readability without sacrificing clarity.

```
let name = "Swift"      // Inferred as String
let count = 10          // Inferred as Int
```

This doesn't mean types are loosely enforced—Swift still maintains static type checking. The language only allows inference when the compiler can determine the correct type unambiguously. This distinction prevents common mistakes found in dynamically typed environments.

Type Constraints: Keeping Code Honest

When writing generic functions or types, constraints ensure the code applies only to compatible data. These constraints clarify intent and eliminate unexpected behavior during compilation.

```swift
func sum<T: Numeric>(_ a: T, _ b: T) -> T {
    return a + b
}
```

Here, the constraint `T: Numeric` ensures that only types conforming to `Numeric` (such as `Int`, `Double`, etc.) can be passed. Without this, misuse could lead to ambiguous or unsafe operations.

Developers can also apply multiple constraints using `where` clauses, such as:

```swift
func combine<T, U>(a: T, b: U) where T: CustomStringConvertible, U: Equatable
{
    print(a.description)
}
```

This style of constraint-based programming allows developers to create generic functions that are tightly scoped and easily testable.

Protocol-Oriented Programming

Moving Beyond Inheritance

Traditional object-oriented programming leans heavily on class hierarchies and inheritance. While useful in some contexts, inheritance chains can lead to rigid designs and unpredictable side effects due to shared state.

Swift promotes an alternative model: **protocol-oriented programming**. This approach uses protocols to define capabilities, which are then adopted by structs, classes, or enums.

```
protocol Authenticatable {
    func authenticate() -> Bool
}
```

Any type that conforms to `Authenticatable` is required to implement the `authenticate` method, regardless of whether it is a class, struct, or enum.

Composing Behavior with Protocols

Protocols allow developers to break complex behavior into focused, testable parts. Instead of relying on a base class to provide all behavior, smaller protocols can be composed together:

```
protocol Identifiable {
    var id: String { get }
}
```

```
protocol Timestamped {
    var createdAt: Date { get }
}
```

These can then be combined:

```
struct User: Identifiable, Timestamped {
    let id: String
    let createdAt: Date
}
```

This model makes it easy to build types that share functionality without locking them into rigid inheritance trees. It also makes unit testing and mocking simpler because protocols can be easily swapped out with mock implementations.

Default Implementations via Protocol Extensions

Swift supports protocol extensions, which allow developers to provide default behavior while still allowing for overrides when needed.

```
extension Authenticatable {
    func authenticate() -> Bool {
        return true
    }
}
```

This lets developers write flexible, scalable systems where new conforming types automatically benefit from shared implementations.

Practical Generics and Associated Types

Writing Reusable Components

Generics allow developers to write flexible, reusable code components without losing type safety. Instead of writing multiple versions of a function or struct for different data types, a generic type parameter can be used.

```
struct Box<T> {
    let value: T
}
```

This approach enables consistent behavior across different types while minimizing code duplication.

Function-Level Generics

Generic functions can be written to work across multiple types while maintaining the same structure. For instance, a sorting function may be written like this:

```swift
func areEqual<T: Equatable>(_ a: T, _ b: T) -> Bool {
    return a == b
}
```

Here, `T` is restricted to types that conform to `Equatable`, ensuring the `==` operator will behave correctly.

Associated Types in Protocols

When protocols need to work with unknown or variable types, Swift allows the use of `associatedtype` to create placeholder types that will be specified later by conforming types.

```swift
protocol Storage {
    associatedtype Item
    func store(_ item: Item)
    func retrieve() -> Item
}
```

A conforming struct could define the specific type to be used:

```swift
struct StringStorage: Storage {
    func store(_ item: String) { print("Stored \(item)") }
    func retrieve() -> String { return "Data" }
}
```

This enables developers to write protocols that are highly flexible yet still type-safe, avoiding the pitfalls of loosely typed interfaces.

Type Erasure for Generic Protocols

In some situations, protocols with associated types or self requirements cannot be used as stand-alone types. Type erasure techniques allow developers to abstract the underlying type while preserving its interface.

This is useful when you want to store heterogeneous types conforming to the same protocol:

```swift
struct AnyStorage<T>: Storage {
    private let _store: (T) -> Void
    private let _retrieve: () -> T

    init<S: Storage>(_ storage: S) where S.Item == T {
        _store = storage.store
        _retrieve = storage.retrieve
    }

    func store(_ item: T) { _store(item) }
    func retrieve() -> T { _retrieve() }
}
```

Though not commonly needed for small apps, this pattern becomes valuable in framework development or modular architectures where abstraction boundaries are critical.

Error Handling the Smart Way

Managing errors effectively is one of the key pillars of robust software development. Swift offers a powerful and flexible error handling system built directly into its syntax and design philosophy. Rather than treating errors as exceptions to be caught reactively, Swift encourages developers to anticipate, isolate, and handle potential failure points with care. This section covers how to throw, catch, and manage errors thoughtfully, how to create and structure custom errors, and how to architect resilient user experiences through consistent and transparent error recovery.

Throwing, Catching, and Managing Gracefully

Understanding Swift's Error Model

Swift uses a structured approach to error handling that avoids runtime surprises and enforces clarity at compile time. Errors in Swift are represented by types that conform to the `Error` protocol. Functions that can produce errors must be explicitly marked with the `throws` keyword, making the potential for failure visible at the call site.

```
enum FileError: Error {
    case notFound
    case unreadable
    case permissionDenied
}

func readFile(_ path: String) throws -> String {
    guard path != "" else { throw FileError.notFound }
```

```
    return "File contents"
}
```

This level of transparency ensures developers confront possible failure instead of ignoring it, and gives calling code the tools to handle problems with precision.

Using do, try, and catch

Swift's do-try-catch syntax provides a structured way to attempt an operation and handle errors based on their type.

```
do {
    let result = try readFile("notes.txt")
    print(result)
} catch FileError.notFound {
    print("The file was not found.")
} catch FileError.permissionDenied {
    print("Access denied.")
} catch {
    print("An unexpected error occurred: \(error)")
}
```

Each catch block can handle a specific error case, and Swift ensures all errors are caught or explicitly passed up the call stack. This makes unhandled error scenarios almost impossible without intentionally ignoring them, which is not recommended in production-grade code.

Optional try? and Forced try!

For cases where you're willing to accept a nil in the event of failure, try? provides a shorthand way of attempting a throwing function and returning nil if it fails.

```
let file = try? readFile("missing.txt")
```

This is useful for non-critical operations where fallback behavior is easy to define. However, try! is used to assert that an error will never occur, and if it does, the app will crash. This should be used with extreme caution and only when you're absolutely certain the function won't fail.

```
let file = try! readFile("valid.txt")
```

Custom Errors and Recovery Patterns

Defining Meaningful Error Types

Using enums for error definitions encourages well-structured, descriptive failure modes. This keeps error handling clear and testable. Each error case can optionally carry associated values for deeper context.

```
enum LoginError: Error {
    case invalidCredentials
    case serverUnavailable(code: Int)
}
```

This approach allows error cases to provide more than just labels—they can also carry metadata that improves recovery logic or user feedback.

Grouping Errors by Domain

Separating error types by domain helps modularize error handling. Instead of using one global error enum for an entire app, different modules can define their own errors:

- NetworkError for networking

- DatabaseError for local storage

- `UserInputError` for validation

This modular strategy also makes testing easier, since different tests can focus on different types of failure without overlapping concerns.

Recovery Through Fallbacks and Retries

In real-world applications, handling errors should include a recovery plan. For example, a failed network request may trigger a retry with exponential backoff, while a user authentication failure might offer a reset password option.

```swift
func fetchDataWithRetry(url: String, attempts: Int = 3) {
    for attempt in 1...attempts {
        do {
            let data = try fetchData(from: url)
            print("Data received: \(data)")
            return
        } catch {
            print("Attempt \(attempt) failed.")
            if attempt == attempts {
                print("All attempts exhausted.")
            }
        }
    }
}
```

This design builds resilience directly into the code, helping it recover from temporary failures without crashing or degrading the user experience.

Building Resilient User Flows with Swift Errors

Anticipating User-Facing Failures

Effective error handling is not just about keeping the code from crashing; it's about guiding the user through uncertain outcomes. When errors occur, users should be informed clearly and given a path forward. This could mean:

- Offering retry buttons after a failed request

- Displaying human-readable messages instead of raw technical descriptions

- Logging error details quietly while offering a clean interface

Example:

```
switch loginResult {
case .success(let user):
   showWelcomeScreen(for: user)
case .failure(let error):
   if let loginError = error as? LoginError {
      switch loginError {
      case .invalidCredentials:
         showAlert("Incorrect username or password.")
      case .serverUnavailable(let code):
         showAlert("Server error \(code). Please try again later.")
      }
   } else {
      showAlert("Something went wrong. Please contact support.")
   }
}
```

This type of structured response handling gives users control even when things go wrong, and demonstrates professional care in app development.

Logging and Monitoring

Resilient systems are built with observability in mind. Even when an error is caught and managed gracefully, it should still be logged. Whether using basic print statements during development or sending error data to a monitoring service in production, this information is essential for debugging and continuous improvement.

```
catch {
    logError(error, context: "File download failed")
    showAlert("We couldn't load your file. Please try again.")
}
```

Adding context to each log makes it easier to trace the root cause when reviewing errors later.

Testing for Fault Tolerance

Well-handled errors are often invisible to users, but they need to be visible to testers. Automated tests should simulate error conditions intentionally to ensure that app behavior remains consistent.

```
func testFileReadThrows() {
    XCTAssertThrowsError(try readFile(""))
}
```

This kind of testing validates not just functionality, but also user trust. A well-tested app handles failure as predictably as it handles success.

Part II
Architecture That Doesn't Break in Production

Modular App Design with Swift

Modular architecture is a practical approach to building applications that are organized, maintainable, and scalable over time. Instead of crafting one large, tightly coupled codebase, modular design encourages developers to structure their applications as independent, reusable units of functionality. This makes it easier to maintain, test, and scale an application without introducing unnecessary technical debt or regression risks. In Swift, modular design can be effectively implemented using tools like Xcode's workspace structure, Swift Package Manager, and techniques such as dependency injection and feature isolation.

This section explores how to break down app features into logical layers, integrate reusable patterns like feature toggles and dependency injection, and construct scalable modules using Swift and Xcode.

Breaking Down Features into Logical Layers

The Purpose of Layering

Applications often suffer when the code for business logic, data handling, and user interface becomes tangled. Modular design begins with clean separation. A layered architecture separates concerns by their function rather than their implementation order. This minimizes dependencies and makes each part of the codebase easier to manage.

Common Layers in Swift Applications

A well-layered application generally includes the following parts:

- **Presentation Layer:** Handles user interface and interaction.

- **Business Logic Layer (Use Cases):** Contains rules that process user actions or external inputs.

- **Data Layer:** Manages data from local storage or remote services.

- **Service Layer:** Provides access to external dependencies such as APIs or system utilities.

Each layer should have a clear contract, often expressed using protocols, to isolate behavior and encourage testability.

```swift
// Data Layer
protocol UserRepository {
    func fetchUser(id: String) -> User?
}

// Business Logic Layer
class GetUserUseCase {
    private let repository: UserRepository

    init(repository: UserRepository) {
        self.repository = repository
    }

    func execute(id: String) -> User? {
        return repository.fetchUser(id: id)
    }
}
```

By isolating logic this way, developers can make changes within one layer without disrupting the rest of the application.

Dependency Injection, Feature Toggles, and Reusability

Why Dependency Injection Matters

Tight coupling between components leads to systems that are difficult to maintain or test. Dependency injection (DI) allows components to receive the dependencies they need from the outside rather than creating them internally. This makes code more modular and test-friendly.

There are three primary approaches to dependency injection:

- **Constructor Injection** (preferred for non-optional dependencies)

- **Property Injection** (when a dependency may be optional or delayed)

- **Method Injection** (useful in certain unit testing contexts)

Example using constructor injection:

```swift
class LoginService {
    private let apiClient: APIClient

    init(apiClient: APIClient) {
        self.apiClient = apiClient
    }

    func login(username: String, password: String) {
        apiClient.sendLoginRequest(username: username, password: password)
    }
}
```

Using dependency injection frameworks is not always necessary. In Swift, simplicity and manual injection are often more maintainable for small to mid-size projects.

Feature Toggles for Controlled Rollouts

Feature toggles, also known as feature flags, are a method for enabling or disabling application features without deploying new code. This allows developers to test new functionality safely or gradually expose it to a subset of users.

A common approach is to create a configuration system that can enable or disable features at runtime:

```swift
struct FeatureFlags {
    static var isNewCheckoutEnabled: Bool {
        return UserDefaults.standard.bool(forKey: "newCheckout")
    }
}
```

In combination with remote configuration or environment-specific builds, feature toggles enable continuous delivery practices without sacrificing control over the user experience.

Building for Reuse

Designing components to be reusable means avoiding hard-coded dependencies and keeping concerns well-separated. Modules that expose protocols instead of concrete types can be reused across different parts of the application or even across different projects.

```swift
protocol AnalyticsLogger {
    func logEvent(name: String, parameters: [String: Any]?)
}
```

Later, this protocol can be implemented by different services (e.g., a local logger, a third-party tool) without changing the business logic.

This flexibility makes it easier to swap out implementations and encourages modular thinking by default.

Creating Scalable Modules in Xcode

Organizing with Xcode Workspaces and Projects

In larger applications, it becomes impractical to place everything in a single project file. Xcode workspaces allow multiple projects or Swift packages to coexist and interact. You can split your application into independent modules like:

- **CoreModule** – Reusable utilities, extensions, and shared types.

- **AuthModule** – Handles all authentication-related features.

- **NetworkingModule** – Manages API requests and decoding.

- **UIModule** – UI components like custom views or reusable cells.

Using multiple targets and custom schemes in Xcode, you can structure your application so that each module compiles independently. This speeds up build times and isolates potential regressions.

Swift Package Manager for Dependency Isolation

Swift Package Manager (SPM) allows you to define standalone modules with their own dependencies and logic. Each module has a manifest file (`Package.swift`) that describes its targets and dependencies.

Example of a package with separate modules:

```
// Package.swift

let package = Package(
    name: "MyAppModules",
    platforms: [.iOS(.v14)],
    products: [
```

```
    .library(name: "Networking", targets: ["Networking"]),
    .library(name: "Authentication", targets: ["Authentication"])
  ],
  targets: [
    .target(name: "Networking"),
    .target(name: "Authentication", dependencies: ["Networking"])
  ]
)
```

This structure keeps your codebase organized and ensures a clear separation between feature areas.

Example: Building a Modular Feature

Let's say you want to create a modular login feature:

1. **NetworkingModule** handles the API request for login.

2. **AuthModule** contains the logic for validating input and triggering the request.

3. **UIModule** provides a `LoginViewController` and UI elements.

4. **AppModule** ties everything together using dependency injection and navigation logic.

This modularization allows you to independently test each module, replace one without affecting others, and onboard new developers more efficiently.

MVC, MVVM, and Coordinators in Practice

Architectural patterns guide how we structure applications and organize responsibilities between components. In Swift development, particularly for iOS, three architectural patterns have proven to be particularly influential: Model-View-Controller (MVC), Model-View-ViewModel (MVVM), and the Coordinator pattern. Each serves a specific purpose and helps in solving common problems such as tight coupling, code repetition, and poor navigation management.

Knowing when and where to apply each pattern is what separates a haphazard app from a maintainable, scalable product. This section focuses on applying these patterns practically, building coordinators to simplify navigation, and understanding the architectural trade-offs developers face in real projects.

When and Where to Use Which Pattern

Model-View-Controller (MVC)

Overview

MVC is the default pattern promoted in many tutorials and official platform examples. It separates concerns into:

- **Model**: The data layer and business logic.

- **View**: The user interface.

- **Controller**: The mediator between model and view.

In theory, each component has a clean responsibility. In practice, however, the controller often becomes bloated with logic not fitting neatly into either the model or view. This has earned it the nickname "Massive View Controller."

When to Use

MVC still serves well in small applications or modules with straightforward flows. It's also useful when rapidly prototyping or working with views that require minimal business logic.

Trade-offs

- **Pros**: Simplicity, quick to implement, ideal for prototyping.

- **Cons**: Controllers can grow too large, making testing and maintenance harder.

Model-View-ViewModel (MVVM)

Overview

MVVM addresses the bloated controller issue by introducing a **ViewModel**, which handles presentation logic and state transformation. This allows the **ViewController** to focus purely on view updates and input handling.

A simple example of a ViewModel:

```
class LoginViewModel {
    var username: String = ""
    var password: String = ""

    var isLoginEnabled: Bool {
        return !username.isEmpty && !password.isEmpty
```

```
    }

    func performLogin(completion: (Bool) -> Void) {
        // Perform login logic
        completion(true)
    }
}
```

When to Use

MVVM is suitable when your view requires state transformation or when you need better test coverage for UI logic. It also plays well with reactive programming tools such as Combine, but doesn't require them.

Trade-offs

- **Pros**: Improved separation of concerns, easier unit testing of UI logic, better scalability.

- **Cons**: Can add complexity in small projects, boilerplate risk if not managed carefully.

Coordinators

Overview

Coordinators are not a replacement for MVC or MVVM—they complement them by moving navigation logic out of the controller. A **Coordinator** manages transitions between screens and encapsulates flow control.

This leads to smaller, more reusable view controllers and enables flows to be tested and reused independently.

Basic example:

```swift
class LoginCoordinator {
    let navigationController: UINavigationController

    init(navigationController: UINavigationController) {
        self.navigationController = navigationController
    }

    func start() {
        let viewModel = LoginViewModel()
        let loginVC = LoginViewController(viewModel: viewModel)
        navigationController.pushViewController(loginVC, animated: true)
    }

    func showSignup() {
        let signupVC = SignupViewController()
        navigationController.pushViewController(signupVC, animated: true)
    }
}
```

When to Use

Coordinators shine when managing complex user flows, especially when multiple view controllers must interact or transitions depend on asynchronous events. They make it easier to handle deep links, onboarding flows, authentication gates, or modal flows.

Trade-offs

- **Pros**: Cleaner navigation logic, increased testability, better flow reusability.

- **Cons**: Slightly more setup and boilerplate, requires discipline to maintain.

Building Coordinators That Simplify Flows

Key Responsibilities

A good coordinator should do the following:

- Create and own view controllers for a specific flow

- Handle user transitions (push, pop, modal, etc.)

- Communicate with other coordinators when needed

You can also define a `Coordinator` protocol to ensure consistent structure:

```
protocol Coordinator {
    var navigationController: UINavigationController { get set }
    func start()
}
```

Then build individual coordinators like:

- `AuthCoordinator` for login/signup flows

- `MainCoordinator` for the main tab interface

- `SettingsCoordinator` for managing user preferences

These can be chained or composed, keeping responsibilities narrow and manageable.

Passing Data Between Coordinators

To pass data between coordinators or view controllers, use delegation or callback closures. Avoid using global state or tightly coupling modules.

Example using a closure:

```
loginViewModel.onLoginSuccess = { [weak self] in
    self?.showHomeScreen()
}
```

This allows flows to be coordinated without having to reference parent view controllers directly.

Real-Life Architectural Decisions and Trade-Offs

Starting Small, Scaling Later

It's tempting to pick the "perfect" pattern upfront. But in most cases, choosing the right pattern is a matter of project size and future expectations. A login screen may be fine with MVC, while a multi-step onboarding experience benefits from MVVM and coordinators.

Start with what's clear, and extract complexity only when needed. Architecture is about trade-offs, not correctness.

Avoiding Overengineering

While abstraction can be powerful, overengineering leads to a codebase that's difficult to navigate. MVVM may reduce controller bloat, but if the ViewModel is just mirroring the controller without adding value, it's unnecessary overhead.

Use the following checkpoints to assess pattern choices:

- **Is the controller hard to test?** → Consider introducing a ViewModel.

- **Is the navigation logic growing too complex?** → Introduce a Coordinator.

- **Is the logic small and contained?** → Stick with MVC.

Combining Patterns

A mature codebase doesn't rely on one pattern alone. Coordinators often coexist with MVVM, and even MVC controllers can be nested inside Coordinator-based flows. Don't treat patterns as dogma—they are tools to solve specific problems.

Team Collaboration Considerations

When working in a team, consistency matters. Define shared architectural guidelines. This makes onboarding easier and reduces confusion. If the project mixes patterns, document where and why each is used.

Networking Without the Pain

Networking in iOS applications can be a challenging task, especially when handling data from external sources like RESTful APIs. Whether you're fetching user data, submitting form details, or syncing app content, a clean, maintainable networking layer is essential to building robust applications. This section explores the critical aspects of networking in iOS using Swift, focusing on practical techniques for working with URLSession, data serialization using Codable, and handling errors and loading states effectively.

URLSession, Codable, and Robust Decoders

URLSession: The Foundation of Networking

URLSession is the primary API for making HTTP requests in iOS. It handles networking tasks such as sending data, receiving data, and managing sessions. It provides a flexible and efficient way to communicate with external services.

A simple URLSession data request might look like this:

```
import Foundation

func fetchData(from url: URL) {
    let task = URLSession.shared.dataTask(with: url) { data, response, error in
        guard let data = data, error == nil else {
            print("Error fetching data: \(error?.localizedDescription ?? "Unknown error")")
            return
        }
```

```
    // Process the data
  }
  task.resume()
}
```

While the basic `URLSession` setup is straightforward, handling complex responses requires a more structured approach, especially when dealing with JSON data.

Codable: Simplifying Data Serialization

In Swift, the `Codable` protocol enables easy encoding and decoding of custom data models. When working with JSON data, `Codable` automates the conversion between JSON objects and native Swift types.

Here's how you can create a `Codable` struct to represent a simple user model:

```
struct User: Codable {
    var id: Int
    var name: String
    var email: String
}
```

To decode the data from a JSON response, you can use `JSONDecoder`:

```
func decodeUserData(from data: Data) {
    let decoder = JSONDecoder()
    do {
        let user = try decoder.decode(User.self, from: data)
        print("User: \(user.name), Email: \(user.email)")
    } catch {
        print("Decoding error: \(error)")
    }
}
```

This ensures that your data is properly parsed into Swift structs, making it more manageable than manually handling raw JSON.

Robust Decoding with Custom Keys

In some cases, the JSON response might not match your struct's property names. To handle this, you can use the `CodingKeys` enum to map JSON keys to your struct properties:

```
struct User: Codable {
    var id: Int
    var name: String
    var email: String

    enum CodingKeys: String, CodingKey {
        case id = "user_id"
        case name = "user_name"
        case email = "user_email"
    }
}
```

This approach keeps your models flexible and maintains clear separation between the external data format and your internal application logic.

API Layer Abstraction Patterns

The Importance of Abstraction

When building apps that rely heavily on external data, it's crucial to separate the networking logic from the rest of the application code. This separation simplifies testing, maintenance, and reuse. By abstracting network calls into a dedicated API layer, you can manage all networking tasks in one place, making your codebase cleaner and more modular.

A simple API manager might look like this:

```swift
class APIManager {
    static let shared = APIManager()

    private init() {}

    func fetchUserData(completion: @escaping (Result<User, Error>) -> Void) {
        guard let url = URL(string: "https://api.example.com/user") else {
            return
        }

        let task = URLSession.shared.dataTask(with: url) { data, response, error in
            if let error = error {
                completion(.failure(error))
                return
            }

            guard let data = data else {
                completion(.failure(NetworkError.noData))
                return
            }

            do {
                let decoder = JSONDecoder()
                let user = try decoder.decode(User.self, from: data)
                completion(.success(user))
            } catch {
                completion(.failure(error))
            }
        }
        task.resume()
```

```
        }
}

enum NetworkError: Error {
    case noData
    case invalidResponse
}
```

In this example, the `APIManager` handles the networking logic and provides an abstraction layer for the rest of the application. This ensures that other components of the app don't need to worry about the technical details of making network requests.

Using Dependency Injection for Flexibility

To ensure your API manager is testable and flexible, consider using **dependency injection**. Instead of having your view controllers or models directly create an instance of the API manager, pass it in via the initializer:

```
class UserViewModel {
    private let apiManager: APIManager

    init(apiManager: APIManager = APIManager.shared) {
        self.apiManager = apiManager
    }

    func fetchUserData() {
        apiManager.fetchUserData { result in
            // Handle result
        }
    }
}
```

This pattern allows you to inject mock API managers during testing, ensuring your code is more modular and easier to test.

Handling API Errors and Loading States Cleanly

Managing Errors with `Result` Type

Handling errors in networking calls is a common source of complexity. The `Result` type in Swift makes it easier to manage success and failure cases by clearly defining success (`.success`) and error (`.failure`) outcomes.

Here's an example using `Result` to handle both API errors and data parsing issues:

```swift
enum NetworkResult<T> {
    case success(T)
    case failure(Error)
}

func fetchData(from url: URL, completion: @escaping (NetworkResult<Data>) -> Void) {
    URLSession.shared.dataTask(with: url) { data, response, error in
        if let error = error {
            completion(.failure(error))
            return
        }

        guard let data = data else {
            completion(.failure(NetworkError.noData))
            return
        }

        completion(.success(data))
    }.resume()
```

}

This pattern simplifies error handling by allowing consumers of the API to handle success and failure cases clearly and concisely.

Loading States and UI Updates

A critical part of handling networking requests is providing feedback to the user during loading states. Users need to know when a request is in progress, and they should be informed of success or failure when the request completes.

Here's a common approach to manage loading states:

```swift
class UserViewModel {
    enum State {
        case idle
        case loading
        case loaded(User)
        case error(Error)
    }

    private(set) var state: State = .idle {
        didSet {
            stateChanged?()
        }
    }

    var stateChanged: (() -> Void)?

    func fetchUserData() {
        state = .loading

        APIManager.shared.fetchUserData { result in
            switch result {
            case .success(let user):
```

```
        self.state = .loaded(user)
      case .failure(let error):
        self.state = .error(error)
      }
    }
  }
}
```

In this example, the `UserViewModel` tracks the loading state and notifies listeners when it changes. By observing the `state` property, the UI can react accordingly (e.g., showing a loading spinner, displaying user data, or presenting an error message).

Best Practices for Handling API Errors

1. **Use Standardized Error Handling**: Create a common error model or enum to ensure consistency throughout the app. This allows you to capture various error scenarios in a uniform way.

2. **Retry Mechanism**: Implement a retry mechanism for failed requests. This can be particularly helpful for transient network issues.

3. **Network Connectivity Check**: Always check for network availability before making a request. You can use libraries like Reachability to detect network connectivity issues early.

4. **Graceful Failure**: When an error occurs, ensure that the app can recover gracefully. For example, you might want to show a user-friendly error message or attempt to recover by fetching cached data.

Data Persistence in the Real World

In the development of modern iOS applications, managing data storage is a critical aspect. Data persistence allows apps to store information locally, ensuring that it is available even after the app is closed or the device is restarted. Effective data persistence strategies not only keep user data intact but also enhance app performance and usability. This section focuses on key methods of data persistence in iOS, including Core Data, lightweight storage solutions like UserDefaults and FileManager, and strategies for building local caches and syncing with remote data sources.

Core Data Essentials (with Performance in Mind)

Understanding Core Data

Core Data is Apple's framework for managing object graphs and persistence. It provides a sophisticated data model layer that enables developers to work with a data model in an object-oriented way while abstracting the complexities of storing and retrieving data. Core Data is ideal for managing complex data structures and relationships between entities.

However, Core Data is not just about storing data. It also provides powerful features such as querying, filtering, and sorting data, making it a go-to choice for many iOS apps. While it is incredibly powerful, it's important to use Core Data efficiently to maintain good app performance, especially when dealing with large datasets.

Core Data Performance Considerations

1. **Use of Background Contexts**: When working with Core Data, it's important to perform heavy data tasks on background threads. If you process large datasets on the main thread, it can lead to a poor user experience due to UI stuttering or app lag. Core Data allows you to create background contexts to manage tasks asynchronously and merge changes back to the main context.

2. **Fetching Strategies**: When fetching data from Core Data, always be mindful of performance. For example, if you need to display a list of records, using `NSFetchRequest` with the `fetchLimit` and `fetchOffset` properties allows you to paginate results and reduce memory usage. Fetching too much data at once can lead to excessive memory usage, which might slow down the app.

3. **Faulting and Lazy Loading**: Core Data uses a concept called "faulting," which means it only loads the data it needs when requested. When working with large datasets, Core Data only fetches the properties of objects that are used, thus minimizing the amount of memory used. Be aware that faulting can lead to issues when accessing properties of objects off-thread or after they have been unloaded.

4. **Data Model Optimization**: To ensure optimal performance, it's crucial to design a data model that fits the needs of the app. Avoid having overly complex relationships, as they can slow down fetches and data manipulation. When designing relationships between entities, always consider the cardinality (one-to-one, one-to-many, many-to-many) and the impact it will have on performance.

5. **Indexing**: Core Data allows you to define indexes on attributes that are frequently queried. This can significantly improve the performance of fetch requests, especially on large datasets. Ensure that attributes used for filtering or sorting are indexed.

Lightweight Storage with UserDefaults and FileManager

UserDefaults: Simple and Fast for Small Data

For storing small amounts of user data, such as preferences, settings, or flags, `UserDefaults` is an ideal choice. It provides a simple key-value store that persists data between app launches. However, `UserDefaults` should not be used for storing sensitive data or large objects.

Here's how you can store and retrieve simple data with `UserDefaults`:

```
// Saving data
UserDefaults.standard.set("John Doe", forKey: "username")
```

```
// Retrieving data
if let username = UserDefaults.standard.string(forKey: "username") {
    print("Hello, \(username)")
}
```

Use Cases for UserDefaults:

- Storing user preferences like theme settings (light/dark mode).

- Saving authentication tokens for session management.

- Tracking small pieces of information like the app version number.

While `UserDefaults` is fast and simple, keep in mind that it is not designed to store large amounts of data. Using it for larger datasets or sensitive information can lead to performance problems and potential security concerns.

FileManager: Managing Files and Directories

When dealing with larger data or non-structured data, `FileManager` provides a better alternative. It allows you to manage files and directories on the file system.

For instance, if you need to store documents or images locally, `FileManager` gives you full control over the file path and how the files are organized.

Example usage of `FileManager` to store and retrieve a file:

```
// Get the documents directory path
let documentsDirectory = FileManager.default.urls(for: .documentDirectory, in: .userDomainMask).first!

// Create a file URL
let fileURL = documentsDirectory.appendingPathComponent("userProfile.txt")

// Saving data to the file
let profileData = "Name: John Doe, Age: 30".data(using: .utf8)!
do {
    try profileData.write(to: fileURL)
    print("File saved!")
} catch {
    print("Error saving file: \(error)")
}

// Reading data from the file
do {
    let savedData = try Data(contentsOf: fileURL)
    if let profileString = String(data: savedData, encoding: .utf8) {
        print("Saved profile: \(profileString)")
    }
} catch {
    print("Error reading file: \(error)")
}
```

Use Cases for FileManager:

- Storing documents, images, or media files.

- Saving serialized data in formats like JSON or XML.

- Caching downloaded files for offline access.

Performance Considerations

Both `UserDefaults` and `FileManager` offer straightforward solutions for lightweight data storage, but there are some performance considerations:

- **UserDefaults** should only be used for small data that doesn't need complex structures. It should not be used for large arrays or dictionaries, as it can negatively affect app performance.

- **FileManager** can handle large files but might be slower compared to databases like Core Data for complex querying or relational data. For large files, consider the file's size and whether it needs to be cached or indexed for faster access.

Building Local Caches and Syncing Strategies

Caching for Improved Performance

Caching is an important strategy in iOS development to improve app performance, especially when dealing with network data. By saving downloaded content locally, you can minimize redundant network requests and provide a better user experience. Caching can be implemented using various techniques, including in-memory caches, file caches, or a combination of both.

For in-memory caching, `NSCache` is a good option. It works similarly to a dictionary but is optimized for caching data. Unlike dictionaries, `NSCache` automatically removes objects from memory when the system runs low on resources.

Here's an example of how you can use NSCache:

```
let imageCache = NSCache<NSString, UIImage>()

func cacheImage(_ image: UIImage, forKey key: String) {
    imageCache.setObject(image, forKey: key as NSString)
}

func getCachedImage(forKey key: String) -> UIImage? {
    return imageCache.object(forKey: key as NSString)
}
```

Syncing Local Data with Remote Servers

Once you've implemented caching, it's crucial to sync the local data with remote servers. This ensures that users have the most up-to-date information while avoiding unnecessary network requests.

Here are a few strategies for syncing data:

1. **Background Syncing**: Implement background tasks to sync data when the app is not actively in use. This can be done using background fetch or push notifications to trigger data syncing.

2. **Incremental Syncing**: Instead of syncing the entire dataset every time, consider syncing only the data that has changed. This can be done using timestamps or change logs to keep track of updates and changes on the server.

3. **Error Handling and Retry Mechanism**: Syncing with remote servers is not always smooth. To handle network failures or server issues, implement a retry mechanism with exponential backoff to avoid overwhelming the server or draining the user's battery.

Part III

Building Features That Work and Scale

SwiftUI for Real-World Interfaces

SwiftUI has revolutionized how developers build user interfaces for iOS, macOS, watchOS, and tvOS. Its declarative syntax allows for cleaner, more concise code, making it easier to build robust, dynamic interfaces. This framework is designed to replace UIKit in many cases, but it's important to understand both its differences from UIKit and the best practices for leveraging SwiftUI in production-grade applications. This section explores SwiftUI in practice, focusing on how it compares to UIKit, how to build reusable views and state-driven UIs, and how to manage navigation and view models efficiently.

How SwiftUI Differs from UIKit—Practically

Declarative vs. Imperative

The key difference between SwiftUI and UIKit lies in their approaches to defining user interfaces. UIKit uses an imperative approach, which requires developers to specify exactly how to update the UI. For example, in UIKit, you manually modify the properties of UI components and update the screen accordingly. This often involves dealing with view controllers, delegates, and other components that make the codebase more complex and harder to manage over time.

On the other hand, SwiftUI embraces a declarative syntax, which simplifies UI code. In SwiftUI, you define the desired state of the UI, and the framework automatically handles updates to the view when the state changes. This removes much of the boilerplate code associated with UI management in UIKit and makes the code more predictable and easier to maintain.

For instance, to create a button in UIKit, you would typically create an instance of `UIButton`, set its properties, add it to a view hierarchy, and implement actions for when the button is pressed. In SwiftUI, the process is more intuitive:

```
Button(action: {

    print("Button pressed")

}) {

    Text("Press Me")

}
```

SwiftUI automatically handles the button's state and updates the UI when needed, without the need for manual state management or event handling.

Dynamic Layouts

Another area where SwiftUI shines over UIKit is its layout system. SwiftUI uses a flexible layout system where views are automatically adjusted based on their content and the available space. In UIKit, you would typically rely on Auto Layout, which requires defining constraints between views. While powerful, Auto Layout can become cumbersome in complex layouts, and mistakes in constraints can lead to hard-to-debug layout issues.

In SwiftUI, layouts are more adaptive. For instance, you can use `VStack`, `HStack`, and `ZStack` to arrange views vertically, horizontally, or on top of each other, respectively. These stacks automatically adjust the layout based on the size of their child views. SwiftUI also provides `GeometryReader` to create custom layouts based on the available space.

```
VStack {

    Text("Top View")

    Text("Bottom View")
```

```
}
```

This declarative layout approach reduces the complexity of creating adaptive and responsive user interfaces.

State Management and Data Binding

State management is another area where SwiftUI simplifies the process compared to UIKit. In UIKit, managing view state often involves a mix of `UIControl` events, delegation, and `NSNotificationCenter` for communication. This can lead to convoluted code that's difficult to maintain as the project grows.

SwiftUI uses a data-binding mechanism that automatically updates the UI when the state changes. With properties like `@State`, `@Binding`, and `@Environment`, you can easily link your view's state to its data model and ensure that changes in the data automatically trigger UI updates.

For example, a simple toggle in SwiftUI:

```
@State private var isOn = false
```

```
var body: some View {

    Toggle("Enable Feature", isOn: $isOn)

}
```

In this example, the state of the `isOn` property is automatically bound to the toggle, and any changes in the state will automatically update the view.

Building Reusable Views and State-Driven UIs

Reusability with Views

In real-world development, creating reusable components is crucial for maintaining a clean, scalable codebase. SwiftUI encourages the creation of reusable views by defining them as simple structs. A SwiftUI view is a lightweight structure that describes its content and layout, and it can be reused across different parts of an application with minimal effort.

For example, creating a reusable card view in SwiftUI might look like this:

```swift
struct CardView: View {

    var title: String

    var subtitle: String


    var body: some View {
        VStack {
            Text(title).font(.headline)

            Text(subtitle).font(.subheadline)
        }
        .padding()

        .background(RoundedRectangle(cornerRadius: 10).fill(Color.blue))
    }
}
```

This `CardView` component can now be used in different parts of the application with varying titles and subtitles:

CardView(title: "Hello", subtitle: "Welcome to SwiftUI")

By separating your UI into small, reusable views, you keep the codebase clean and easy to modify.

State-Driven UI Design

SwiftUI's declarative nature is especially powerful when combined with state-driven UI design. The user interface in SwiftUI reacts directly to changes in the state, making it easy to maintain consistency and ensure the interface reflects the app's current data. With state-driven design, each view is responsible for managing its own state, making the code more modular and easier to maintain.

Here's an example of a state-driven UI where a button's text changes based on user interaction:

```
@State private var buttonText = "Press Me"


var body: some View {

    VStack {

        Button(action: {

            buttonText = "You Pressed Me!"

        }) {

            Text(buttonText)

        }

    }

}
```

As the `buttonText` changes, SwiftUI automatically updates the button's label. This makes it easy to create dynamic UIs without manually managing the view state or performing updates.

Managing Navigation and View Models Properly

Navigation in SwiftUI

Navigation is a fundamental aspect of most apps, and SwiftUI provides a streamlined approach to handle it. Using `NavigationView` and `NavigationLink`, developers can easily manage navigation stacks. The declarative nature of SwiftUI ensures that the navigation state is managed automatically.

For example, to create a basic navigation flow:

```
NavigationView {

    NavigationLink(destination: Text("Detail View")) {

        Text("Go to Detail")

    }

}
```

This simple navigation setup automatically handles pushing and popping views onto the navigation stack. SwiftUI ensures that the navigation state is updated and that the UI reflects the current navigation hierarchy.

For more complex scenarios, such as passing data between views, you can bind the data to the `NavigationLink`:

```
NavigationView {
```

```
NavigationLink(destination: DetailView(data: itemData)) {

    Text("Go to Detail")

}

}
```

View Models and Data Binding

A key principle in SwiftUI is that the UI should always reflect the current state of the data. To implement this, SwiftUI relies heavily on view models, which manage the business logic and data for a view. The view model is responsible for fetching data, performing computations, and providing state to the UI, while the view is responsible for rendering the UI and reacting to changes in state.

In SwiftUI, view models are commonly implemented using `ObservableObject` and `@Published`:

```
class UserProfileViewModel: ObservableObject {

    @Published var userName: String = ""


    func fetchUserData() {

        // Fetch user data from a network or database

        self.userName = "John Doe"

    }

}
```

In the view, the view model is injected and observed for changes:

```swift
struct UserProfileView: View {

    @ObservedObject var viewModel = UserProfileViewModel()


    var body: some View {
        VStack {

            Text(viewModel.userName)

            Button("Fetch User Data") {

                viewModel.fetchUserData()

            }

        }

    }

}
```

By using `ObservableObject` and `@Published`, any changes to the `userName` in the view model automatically trigger UI updates in the `UserProfileView`.

UIKit in Modern Projects

UIKit remains a cornerstone of iOS development despite the rising popularity of SwiftUI. Its rich feature set and flexibility make it an ideal choice for complex applications, especially when it comes to handling intricate UI layouts, animations, and user interactions. For developers working with UIKit, understanding the framework's nuances and how to implement it effectively in modern projects is essential. This section will explore how to handle the `UIViewController` lifecycle, offer useful Auto Layout tips, and discuss best practices for bridging UIKit with SwiftUI cleanly.

UIViewController Lifecycle Done Right

Understanding the View Controller Lifecycle

The `UIViewController` lifecycle is fundamental to managing the view and its interactions in an iOS app. The lifecycle consists of several key phases, and understanding each one is crucial for ensuring your app performs efficiently while maintaining a clean, maintainable codebase.

1. Initialization and Setup

When a `UIViewController` is first created, the `init` method is called. This is where you set up basic properties and dependencies of the view controller. It's important to avoid heavy lifting in this method, as it runs before the view is actually loaded. Instead, use the `viewDidLoad` method for setup that requires the view to be loaded into memory.

2. viewDidLoad

The `viewDidLoad` method is called once the view controller's view has been loaded into memory. This is the ideal place to set up UI elements, initialize data structures, and perform tasks that rely on the view being fully loaded.

```swift
override func viewDidLoad() {
    super.viewDidLoad()
    // Initialize UI components and perform setup
}
```

A common mistake is to assume that the view is ready for interaction in `viewDidLoad`. It's important to remember that while the view is loaded, it may not yet be part of the window's view hierarchy, meaning some actions might not be immediately visible or interactive.

3. viewWillAppear and viewDidAppear

`viewWillAppear` is called just before the view becomes visible, while `viewDidAppear` is called after the view is added to the window's view hierarchy. These methods are useful for tasks such as starting animations or updating the UI based on changes to data.

```swift
override func viewWillAppear(_ animated: Bool) {
    super.viewWillAppear(animated)
    // Prepare the UI before it appears on screen
}
```

```swift
override func viewDidAppear(_ animated: Bool) {
    super.viewDidAppear(animated)
    // Perform actions after the view has appeared
}
```

4. viewWillDisappear and viewDidDisappear

These methods are called when the view is about to disappear and after it disappears. These are ideal for stopping tasks like animations or saving user data before the view is removed from the hierarchy.

```swift
override func viewWillDisappear(_ animated: Bool) {
    super.viewWillDisappear(animated)
    // Stop tasks that need to be halted when the view disappears
}

override func viewDidDisappear(_ animated: Bool) {
    super.viewDidDisappear(animated)
    // Cleanup tasks after the view disappears
}
```

5. Deinitialization

When the view controller is deallocated, the `deinit` method is called. This is where you should clean up any resources like observers, network requests, or other components that were allocated during the controller's lifecycle.

```swift
deinit {
    // Cleanup
}
```

Best Practices for Managing the Lifecycle

To ensure a smooth user experience and minimize memory leaks, it's critical to follow a few best practices when working with the `UIViewController` lifecycle:

- **Avoid heavy computation in lifecycle methods**: Heavy computation should be moved to background threads to keep the UI responsive.

- **Use `viewDidAppear` for animations**: Start animations in `viewDidAppear` because the view is guaranteed to be visible at this point.

- **Balance memory management**: Always remove observers, timers, or network tasks when the view controller is about to disappear or be deallocated.

Auto Layout Tips That Save Time

Leveraging Auto Layout for Responsive Designs

Auto Layout is an essential tool for building flexible, responsive layouts in UIKit. It ensures that UI elements adapt to different screen sizes and orientations. However, for developers new to Auto Layout or those looking to optimize their workflow, it's important to understand some key strategies to save time and reduce complexity.

1. Prioritize Content Compression and Hugging

Content hugging and content compression resistance are critical concepts in Auto Layout. By adjusting the `contentHuggingPriority` and `contentCompressionResistancePriority` of views, you can control how much space a view can take up and how it responds to resizing.

For instance, a label displaying text might need to resist shrinking, so you can set its compression resistance priority higher than its hugging priority:

```
label.setContentCompressionResistancePriority(.required, for: .horizontal)
label.setContentHuggingPriority(.defaultLow, for: .horizontal)
```

This ensures the label doesn't shrink when the container view is resized.

2. Use Stack Views Effectively

`UIStackView` is a powerful tool for managing layouts in UIKit. It allows you to create complex, adaptable layouts with minimal code. Stack views automatically manage spacing between views and adjust based on their content.

For instance, when arranging buttons vertically, you can use a vertical stack view like this:

```
let stackView = UIStackView(arrangedSubviews: [button1, button2, button3])
stackView.axis = .vertical
stackView.spacing = 10
stackView.alignment = .fill
stackView.distribution = .equalSpacing
```

Stack views reduce the need for manually setting constraints between individual views, making the layout more manageable.

3. Leverage Layout Anchors

Instead of writing multiple NSLayoutConstraint lines for each edge of a view, you can use layout anchors to make your constraints more concise. For example:

```
view.topAnchor.constraint(equalTo: superview.topAnchor, constant: 20).isActive = true
view.leadingAnchor.constraint(equalTo: superview.leadingAnchor, constant: 20).isActive = true
```

This improves readability and reduces boilerplate code, especially when you have several constraints.

4. Avoid Overuse of Constraints

While constraints are essential for building adaptive layouts, excessive use of them can lead to performance issues, especially with complex UI hierarchies. Use constraints only when necessary, and prefer `UIStackView` or flexible frames whenever possible.

Tools to Debug Auto Layout

- **Debugging Visuals**: Use Xcode's Auto Layout debug tools, such as the "View Hierarchy Debugger" and the "Constraints Debugging" feature, to identify conflicting or missing constraints.

- **Intrinsic Content Size**: Set appropriate intrinsic content sizes for custom views to avoid unnecessary constraints.

Bridging UIKit and SwiftUI Cleanly

Integration Between UIKit and SwiftUI

As SwiftUI gains traction, it's common for developers to need to integrate it with UIKit, especially in existing projects that are already built using UIKit. Bridging the two frameworks allows developers to take advantage of SwiftUI's declarative syntax and powerful UI components, while still leveraging UIKit's maturity and flexibility in certain areas.

1. Using UIHostingController

`UIHostingController` is a key tool for integrating SwiftUI views into a UIKit-based application. This controller acts as a bridge, allowing you to embed SwiftUI views inside UIKit view controllers.

For example, if you have a SwiftUI `Text` view that you want to display within a UIKit-based view controller:

```
let swiftUIView = Text("Hello, SwiftUI!")
let hostingController = UIHostingController(rootView: swiftUIView)

addChild(hostingController)
view.addSubview(hostingController.view)
hostingController.didMove(toParent: self)
```

This method allows you to integrate any SwiftUI view into your UIKit hierarchy, providing flexibility for hybrid applications.

2. SwiftUI Views in UIKit Hierarchies

If you need to place UIKit views inside a SwiftUI hierarchy, you can use `UIViewControllerRepresentable` or `UIViewRepresentable` to wrap UIKit views and make them available for use in SwiftUI.

For instance, to integrate a `UIImageView` into a SwiftUI view, you can create a custom `UIViewRepresentable`:

```
struct ImageView: UIViewRepresentable {
    let image: UIImage

    func makeUIView(context: Context) -> UIImageView {
        return UIImageView(image: image)
    }

    func updateUIView(_ uiView: UIImageView, context: Context) {
        uiView.image = image
    }
}
```

You can now use this `ImageView` struct directly in your SwiftUI views:

```
ImageView(image: UIImage(named: "exampleImage")!)
```

3. Communicating Between UIKit and SwiftUI

Sometimes, you need to pass data or trigger actions between UIKit and SwiftUI. For this, you can use a combination of `@Binding`, `ObservableObject`, or delegate patterns to manage communication between the two frameworks. For example, you might create an `ObservableObject` in SwiftUI that listens for changes made in UIKit, or use delegate methods to notify UIKit of changes in SwiftUI.

Concurrency with async/await

Concurrency is a critical aspect of modern software development, especially when building applications that rely on responsiveness and performance. With the introduction of `async/await` in Swift, managing concurrency has become more intuitive, safer, and less error-prone. However, as with any powerful tool, developers must understand how to properly harness it to avoid pitfalls such as deadlocks, race conditions, and UI freezes. This section covers structured concurrency, the role of actors and tasks, and strategies to avoid common concurrency issues.

Structured Concurrency Without Shooting Yourself in the Foot

Understanding Structured Concurrency

Structured concurrency in Swift refers to a design pattern where the lifecycle of concurrent tasks is tightly controlled, making it easier to reason about the flow of execution and avoid issues such as dangling tasks or unhandled errors. Unlike the traditional approach where tasks are often executed without clear scope or ownership, structured concurrency ensures that all tasks are bound within a scope and have a predictable lifecycle.

In Swift, this is achieved through the `async/await` syntax, where tasks are initiated and managed in an organized manner. By adopting structured concurrency, you gain better control over task cancellation, error propagation, and the order of execution, which is essential for keeping your app's performance optimal and reliable.

Key Principles of Structured Concurrency

1. **Scope-Limited Tasks**

   Each task is defined within a specific scope, often associated with a function or object. This ensures that the task is only alive as long as the scope exists, which prevents issues like tasks running indefinitely or being left unfinished.

2. **Error Handling**

   With structured concurrency, tasks can propagate errors up the call stack, making it easier to catch and handle exceptions in a centralized way. Swift's `async/await` mechanism integrates seamlessly with `do-catch` blocks, ensuring robust error management without complex callback chains.

3. **Task Grouping**

   Tasks can be grouped together, and the parent task waits for the completion of all child tasks. This makes the flow of concurrent operations more predictable and organized, which is essential when dealing with multiple asynchronous operations that need to complete in a specific order.

4. **Task Cancellation**

   Swift's concurrency model introduces the concept of task cancellation, which allows for more responsive, user-friendly apps. If a user navigates away from a screen, tasks in progress can be canceled to save system resources, improving performance and battery life.

Structured concurrency also provides built-in mechanisms for cancellation and timeout handling, reducing the chances of resource leaks or unfinished operations in your code.

Actors, Tasks, and Escaping Closures

The Role of Actors in Concurrency

Actors are a new type in Swift designed to protect data from concurrent access, ensuring that only one thread can access an actor's mutable state at a time. This effectively prevents data races, a common problem in concurrent programming, where multiple tasks try to modify the same data simultaneously, leading to unpredictable behavior.

An actor encapsulates its mutable state and only allows access to that state through its methods. By default, any access to an actor's state is done asynchronously, ensuring that tasks are serialized and thus preventing race conditions.

```swift
actor Counter {
    private var count = 0

    func increment() {
        count += 1
    }

    func getCount() -> Int {
        return count
    }
}
```

In the example above, the `Counter` actor ensures that increments to the `count` variable are thread-safe and occur in a controlled manner. Even if multiple tasks attempt to access `count` at the same time, they will be queued and handled serially.

Tasks and Escaping Closures

In Swift, tasks are lightweight units of asynchronous work that can be executed concurrently. The `Task` API provides a way to create and manage these units of work.

A common challenge when working with tasks in Swift is handling escaping closures. Escaping closures are closures that outlive the scope of the function they are passed to. In asynchronous code, closures often escape because they are passed to tasks that run outside of the current function scope.

To handle escaping closures safely in the context of `async/await`, you need to ensure that these closures are executed correctly and that any shared resources are protected to avoid concurrency issues.

```swift
func fetchData(completion: @escaping (Data?) -> Void) {
    Task {
        let data = await downloadData()
        completion(data)
    }
}
```

In the example above, the closure `completion` is escaping because it is executed after the `fetchData` function has returned. The `Task` ensures that the work is completed asynchronously while allowing the closure to escape safely.

It's crucial to be mindful of how and where you define escaping closures to prevent unintended side effects, such as accessing shared data without proper synchronization, which can lead to race conditions.

Avoiding Deadlocks, Race Conditions, and UI Freezes

Understanding Deadlocks and How to Avoid Them

A deadlock occurs when two or more tasks wait indefinitely for each other to finish, resulting in a situation where the app is stuck and unable to proceed. This is a common issue when multiple tasks need to access shared resources but are waiting on each other to release those resources.

To avoid deadlocks in Swift, follow these best practices:

1. **Avoid Nested Locks**

   Be careful when acquiring multiple locks in nested tasks. If Task A holds Lock 1 and waits for Lock 2, and Task B holds Lock 2 and waits for Lock 1, a deadlock will occur. Instead, try to acquire locks in a consistent order.

2. **Use Task Priorities**

   Swift allows you to assign priorities to tasks, ensuring that tasks with higher priority are executed first. By setting task priorities appropriately, you reduce the chance of deadlocks, as lower-priority tasks can be deferred and don't block higher-priority tasks.

3. **Non-blocking Calls**

   Always ensure that tasks are non-blocking. If a task is expected to block for any reason, make sure it is run asynchronously on a background queue and does not lock the main thread.

Preventing Race Conditions

Race conditions occur when multiple tasks concurrently modify shared data without proper synchronization. This leads to inconsistent or incorrect results. In Swift, the actor model helps prevent race conditions by serializing access to mutable state. However, in situations where you're not using actors, you must ensure proper synchronization mechanisms are in place.

Here are some strategies to prevent race conditions:

1. **Serial Queues**

   If you need to manage access to shared data, use serial queues to ensure that only one task accesses the data at a time. For example, you can use a `DispatchQueue` with `.serial` to serialize access to resources.

2. **Locks**

   Swift provides `NSLock`, `NSRecursiveLock`, and other lock mechanisms that can be used to synchronize access to shared data. However, be cautious about using locks excessively, as they can introduce deadlocks if

3. **Atomic Properties**
   When working with basic data types like integers or booleans, you can use atomic properties that ensure safe reading and writing in a multi-threaded environment.

```swift
var count = 0
let lock = NSLock()

func incrementCount() {
    lock.lock()
    count += 1
    lock.unlock()
}
```

Preventing UI Freezes

One of the most common issues when working with concurrency is freezing the UI. This occurs when long-running tasks, like network calls or heavy computations, are executed on the main thread. The main thread is responsible for updating the UI, and if it's blocked by a task, the user interface becomes unresponsive.

To prevent UI freezes, follow these guidelines:

1. **Offload Heavy Work to Background Threads**
   Always execute time-consuming tasks, such as file I/O, network requests, or data processing, on background threads. In Swift, you can use `DispatchQueue.global` for this purpose:

```swift
DispatchQueue.global(qos: .background).async {
    // Time-consuming task
    DispatchQueue.main.async {
```

```
    // Update UI after task completion
  }
}
```

2. **Use async/await for Readable Code**

   Swift's `async/await` makes it easier to offload tasks to background threads without blocking the UI. For example:

```
async {
  let data = await downloadData()
  // Update UI on the main thread
  DispatchQueue.main.async {
    updateUI(with: data)
  }
}
```

3. **Throttle or Debounce UI Updates**

   When handling frequent UI updates, such as during animations or scrolling, use throttling or debouncing techniques to limit the number of updates. This ensures that the UI remains responsive without unnecessary processing.

Reactive Programming with Combine

Reactive programming has significantly changed the way developers approach data handling and user interface (UI) updates. With the introduction of the Combine framework in Swift, developers can adopt a more declarative approach to managing asynchronous events and streamlining UI interactions. Through the use of publishers, subscribers, and operators, Combine enables powerful and efficient handling of real-time data. In this section, we explore the foundational concepts of reactive programming with Combine, from understanding publishers and subscribers to effectively integrating Combine into an MVVM architecture. Additionally, we'll cover best practices for memory management and task cancellation to ensure stable and performant applications.

Publishers, Subscribers, and Chaining Like a Pro

Understanding Publishers and Subscribers

At the heart of Combine is the concept of *publishers* and *subscribers*. Publishers are entities that emit values over time. These values can be of any type, including data, events, or even errors. Subscribers, on the other hand, are responsible for receiving the values that a publisher emits. When combined, these components form the backbone of reactive programming, allowing data to flow seamlessly through an app's layers.

Publishers

Publishers emit a stream of values over time, and they come in various forms. Some publishers emit a single value and complete, while others emit multiple values or even an infinite sequence. The key to understanding Combine is recognizing that publishers are *asynchronous* and can send values at any time, making them perfect for handling events like network responses, user input, or changes in application state.

There are a variety of publishers, such as:

- `Just`: Emits a single value and completes immediately.

- `PassthroughSubject`: Can emit values at any time and allows external code to send values into the stream.

- `CurrentValueSubject`: Similar to `PassthroughSubject` but maintains the latest value and provides a way to retrieve it at any time.

- `NotificationCenter.Publisher`: Publishes system notifications.

```
let publisher = Just("Hello, Combine!")
publisher.sink { value in
    print(value)
}
```

In the above example, the `Just` publisher emits a single value and completes. The subscriber listens for this value and prints it when received.

Subscribers

Subscribers listen to publishers and respond to the values emitted. A subscriber is typically associated with a closure that defines what to do with the incoming data. For example, you might use the `.sink` method, which provides closures for receiving a value and handling completion or errors.

```
let subscription = publisher.sink(
    receiveValue: { value in
```

```
    print("Received value: \(value)")
  },
  receiveCompletion: { completion in
    switch completion {
    case .finished:
      print("Subscription finished successfully.")
    case .failure(let error):
      print("Subscription failed with error: \(error)")
    }
  }
)
```

A key point to remember is that a subscriber will only start receiving values once it has subscribed to a publisher. Therefore, managing subscriptions is crucial to ensuring efficient resource usage and avoiding unnecessary computations.

Chaining Operators for Powerful Data Transformation

Combine shines when it comes to chaining multiple operators together to create complex data pipelines. Operators allow you to transform, filter, or combine data streams in a clean and functional way. Some commonly used operators include:

- `map`: Transforms each value emitted by the publisher.

- `filter`: Allows values to pass through only if they meet certain conditions.

- `flatMap`: Flattens multiple publishers into one by transforming a value into a new publisher.

- `combineLatest`: Combines the latest values from multiple publishers into one stream.

```
let numbersPublisher = [1, 2, 3, 4, 5].publisher

numbersPublisher
    .map { $0 * 2 }
    .filter { $0 > 5 }
    .sink { value in
        print(value) // Prints 6, 8, 10
    }
```

By chaining operators together, developers can compose intricate workflows for managing events, transforming data, and handling side effects—all in a concise, readable manner. This enables a declarative approach to managing application state and events.

Integrating Combine into MVVM

Understanding MVVM Architecture

Model-View-ViewModel (MVVM) is a design pattern that separates concerns in an application, making it easier to test and maintain. In MVVM, the View is responsible for presenting data, the Model contains business logic and data, and the ViewModel acts as a bridge that processes and formats the data from the Model to make it consumable for the View.

When integrating Combine into MVVM, Combine's publishers and subscribers become an excellent fit for managing data flow between the ViewModel and the View.

ViewModel and Combine

In a Combine-powered MVVM architecture, the ViewModel acts as the publisher. It exposes properties via Combine's publishers that the View subscribes to. Whenever the data in the ViewModel changes, the publishers emit new values, and the View automatically updates. This removes the need for manual state management and allows for a fully reactive data flow.

```swift
class ViewModel: ObservableObject {
    @Published var data: String = ""

    func fetchData() {
        // Simulate network request
        Just("Hello, Combine MVVM!")
            .delay(for: .seconds(2), scheduler: DispatchQueue.main)
            .sink { [weak self] value in
                self?.data = value
            }
            .store(in: &cancellables)
    }
}
```

In the code above, the `ViewModel` is an `ObservableObject`, and the `data` property is marked with `@Published`. This means that any change to `data` will automatically notify subscribers (typically the View) to update the UI.

Binding the View to the ViewModel

The View subscribes to the ViewModel's published properties, allowing it to react to any changes. SwiftUI, for instance, uses `@ObservedObject` or `@StateObject` to subscribe to the ViewModel's publishers. This ensures that when data changes, the View is automatically updated.

```swift
struct ContentView: View {
    @StateObject private var viewModel = ViewModel()

    var body: some View {
        VStack {
            Text(viewModel.data)
            Button("Fetch Data") {
```

```
            viewModel.fetchData()
        }
      }
      .onReceive(viewModel.$data) { newData in
        print("Received new data: \(newData)")
      }
    }
  }
}
```

Here, `@StateObject` binds the ViewModel to the View, and whenever the `data` property changes, the View updates automatically, ensuring the UI is always in sync with the underlying model.

Cancellation and Memory Management Done Right

Handling Cancellations with Combine

In reactive programming, it's important to handle cancellation properly. Unnecessary work should be canceled to prevent memory leaks and improve app performance. Combine allows you to manage cancellations through the use of `Cancellable` objects, which are returned when you subscribe to a publisher.

```
var cancellables = Set<AnyCancellable>()

let publisher = Just("Hello, Combine!")
publisher
  .sink { value in
    print(value)
  }
  .store(in: &cancellables)
```

In this example, the `store(in:)` method adds the subscription to a `Set` of `Cancellable` objects. This allows you to cancel subscriptions when no longer needed, which is critical in long-running or resource-intensive tasks.

You can cancel all subscriptions by calling `cancellables.removeAll()`, or cancel a specific subscription using `cancel()` on the `Cancellable` object itself.

Memory Management with Combine

Memory management in reactive programming is crucial, as subscriptions can easily lead to retain cycles or memory leaks if not managed properly. When a publisher sends values to a subscriber, it's important that the subscriber doesn't unintentionally retain the publisher (or vice versa), as this can prevent deallocation of objects.

To prevent retain cycles, Combine uses the `weak` and `unowned` keywords. Additionally, subscribing to publishers in the right places (such as ViewModels or managers) and cancelling subscriptions appropriately helps to keep memory usage efficient.

```
publisher
    .sink(receiveValue: { [weak self] value in
        self?.handleValue(value)
    })
    .store(in: &cancellables)
```

In this example, `weak self` ensures that the `ViewModel` (or any object) does not retain the subscription, preventing a strong reference cycle. This practice ensures that once the `ViewModel` is deallocated, the subscription will also be cancelled, thus preventing memory leaks.

Working with App Lifecycle and System Events

Understanding the app lifecycle and how to handle system events is crucial for building robust iOS applications. The iOS app lifecycle defines the stages an app goes through during its execution, from launching to termination. The system events, such as background tasks and notifications, are integral for maintaining a responsive and efficient app. This section explores the key components of managing the app lifecycle, handling background tasks, and dealing with deep linking and universal links to ensure seamless user experiences.

SceneDelegate, AppDelegate, and Launch Flows

The Role of AppDelegate

The `AppDelegate` class is traditionally responsible for handling global app events, such as application launch, state transitions, and push notifications. Although it's still a key part of iOS app development, its role has been evolving with the introduction of the `SceneDelegate` in later versions of iOS.

In earlier versions of iOS, `AppDelegate` was the primary entry point for the app. It was responsible for handling the following system events:

- **App Launch**: The app's entry point, triggered when the app is opened.

- **State Transitions**: Managing changes in the app's state (active, background, etc.).

- **Push Notifications**: Handling incoming push notifications.

With the introduction of `SceneDelegate`, the responsibility for managing scenes (instances of the app's user interface) was shifted from `AppDelegate` to `SceneDelegate`. However, `AppDelegate` still plays a crucial role, particularly for app-level behaviors that aren't tied to specific scenes.

SceneDelegate and Managing App UI

`SceneDelegate` is introduced in iOS 13 and is tasked with managing individual scenes or windows of the app. Each scene corresponds to a specific user interface, allowing for multitasking capabilities like multiple windows on iPadOS. Scene management includes:

- **Scene Lifecycle**: The scene lifecycle manages events such as when a scene enters the foreground or goes to the background.

- **Scene Sessions**: If the app supports multiple scenes (like on iPadOS), `SceneDelegate` handles each session independently.

- **User Interface**: It is also responsible for setting up the user interface and transitioning between different states of the app's UI.

The methods in `SceneDelegate` include:

- `scene(_:willConnectTo:options:)`: Called when a scene is first created or connected.

- `sceneDidBecomeActive(_:)`: Called when the scene enters the foreground.

- `sceneDidEnterBackground(_:)`: Called when the scene goes into the background.

- `sceneWillResignActive(_:)`: Called when the scene is about to lose focus.

```
func sceneDidBecomeActive(_ scene: UIScene) {
    // Restart tasks that were paused when the scene was inactive
}
```

This separation of responsibilities allows iOS to handle multiple windows or scenes more effectively, improving multitasking and overall usability.

The Launch Flow: A Combined Effort of AppDelegate and SceneDelegate

At the start of an app launch, the `AppDelegate` is invoked first, and then the app initializes scenes via the `SceneDelegate`. The `AppDelegate` handles broader application-level events, like setting up push notification configurations, while the `SceneDelegate` manages the lifecycle of individual scenes. The flow of control typically works like this:

1. **App Launch**: `AppDelegate`'s `application(_:didFinishLaunchingWithOptions:)` is triggered.

2. **Scene Creation**: After the app is initialized, the `SceneDelegate` takes over to create and manage the initial scene.

3. **Scene Activation**: If the app has multiple scenes, they are created and activated by the `SceneDelegate`.

```
func application(_ application: UIApplication, didFinishLaunchingWithOptions
launchOptions: [UIApplication.LaunchOptionsKey : Any]?) -> Bool {
    // App setup logic here
    return true
}
```

Handling Background Tasks and Notifications

Background Tasks: Managing Time-Intensive Operations

Handling background tasks efficiently is crucial for ensuring a responsive app experience. iOS provides several mechanisms for apps to perform tasks in the background, including background fetch and long-running background tasks.

- **Background Fetch**: Allows apps to periodically fetch data while running in the background. The system decides when to trigger this, based on various factors such as network availability and battery life.

- **Background Audio**: For apps that play audio in the background, iOS provides the ability to keep the app running while the audio continues.

- **Background Location**: Apps that use location services can continue updating the user's location even when the app is not in the foreground.

- **Silent Push Notifications**: Allows apps to receive push notifications without updating the UI, which is ideal for background data sync.

Implementing Background Tasks

To handle background tasks, developers must configure the app with the appropriate capabilities and use the appropriate APIs to manage these tasks. For example, a background fetch task is typically initiated by implementing the following method in `AppDelegate`:

```
func application(_ application: UIApplication,
performFetchWithCompletionHandler completionHandler: @escaping
(UIBackgroundFetchResult) -> Void) {
    // Fetch data in the background
    fetchDataFromServer { success in
        completionHandler(success ? .newData : .noData)
    }
}
```

This method allows the app to perform a data fetch when triggered by the system, ensuring the app can sync data even when the user is not actively interacting with it.

Handling Notifications

Push notifications are a powerful way to keep users engaged with your app, even when it is not actively running in the foreground. iOS offers a variety of notification types, including:

- **Local Notifications**: Notifications triggered within the app based on specific user interactions or events.

- **Push Notifications**: Sent from a server to the device to alert the user about important updates.

In order to manage push notifications effectively, apps must register for notifications and implement methods to handle them. For instance, in `AppDelegate`, the method to register for push notifications might look like this:

```
func application(_ application: UIApplication,
didRegisterForRemoteNotificationsWithDeviceToken deviceToken: Data) {
    // Register device token for push notifications
    PushNotificationManager.shared.registerDeviceToken(deviceToken)
```

```
}
```

When a push notification is received, the app can handle it with methods like `application(_:didReceiveRemoteNotification:fetchCompletionHandler:)`, allowing you to process the notification's payload and update the app's UI or perform background operations accordingly.

Deep Linking and Universal Links That Work Consistently

Understanding Deep Linking

Deep linking allows you to direct users to specific content or functionality within your app. Deep links are URLs that open an app to a particular location, making navigation easier and more intuitive. There are two primary types of deep links:

- **Custom Scheme Links**: A scheme-based link (e.g., `myapp://some/path`) that opens an app when clicked. These links are specific to your app and must be configured in the app's settings.

- **Universal Links**: URLs that are mapped to both a web page and an app. When the user clicks the link, iOS first checks if the app is installed. If the app is installed, it opens; if not, it opens the URL in a browser.

Implementing Universal Links

Universal links offer a more seamless experience, ensuring that users are always directed to the correct app or webpage based on the context. Setting up universal links involves a few steps:

1. **Creating an Apple App Site Association (AASA) File**: This file is hosted on the web server and tells iOS which URLs should open your app.

2. **Configuring Your App**: Your app must support universal links by specifying the associated domains in the app's capabilities.

```swift
func application(_ application: UIApplication, continue userActivity:
NSUserActivity, restorationHandler: @escaping ([UIUserActivityRestoring]?) ->
Void) {
    if userActivity.activityType == NSUserActivityTypeBrowsingWeb {
        // Handle the universal link
    }
}
```

With universal links, iOS will open your app directly when the user clicks a URL associated with your app, leading to a specific screen or piece of content.

Deep Linking with Custom URL Schemes

Custom URL schemes are typically used for directing users from one app to another or to open specific content within the app. For instance, if you want to open a specific screen in your app, you can define a custom URL scheme, such as `myapp://path/to/content`.

To handle these custom links, you'll need to implement methods in `AppDelegate` to process the incoming URL:

```swift
func application(_ application: UIApplication, open url: URL, options:
[UIApplication.OpenURLOptionsKey : Any] = [:]) -> Bool {
    if url.scheme == "myapp" {
        // Handle deep link
    }
    return true
}
```

Custom URL schemes offer more control over how external apps interact with your app, but universal links provide a more user-friendly and consistent experience.

Part IV
Polish, Debug, and Deploy

Debugging Swift Code with Intention

Debugging is an essential skill for every developer. When building applications in Swift, using the right tools and techniques to identify, analyze, and resolve issues effectively can significantly enhance the development process. Debugging isn't just about fixing bugs; it's about understanding the flow of your code, the environment in which it runs, and how to ensure that every part of your application performs as expected. In this section, we'll explore strategies for mastering debugging in Xcode, including powerful features like symbolic breakpoints, logging strategies, and crash tracing. With the right techniques, you can debug Swift code with precision, minimizing issues and improving the quality of your applications.

Xcode Debugger Mastery

The Xcode debugger is one of the most powerful tools available for debugging Swift code. Mastering this tool requires understanding its features and knowing when and how to use them to identify and resolve issues in your code.

Understanding the Debugger Interface

When you run your application in Xcode, the debugger automatically becomes available. The debugger provides a wealth of information about your app's state, including variable values, the call stack, and other runtime details that can help you identify where things are going wrong. The key components of the debugger interface include:

- **Debug Area**: This is where you'll find the console and variable watches. It provides information about the execution of your app, including any errors or warnings.

- **Breakpoints**: These are used to pause the app's execution at specific points in the code. Breakpoints allow you to inspect variables and the flow of execution at precise moments in your program.

- **Call Stack**: The call stack is a list of all the methods and functions that have been called to get to the current point in the code. Reviewing the call stack can help you understand how your app reached its current state.

Step-by-Step Debugging with Breakpoints

Breakpoints are the primary tool in debugging, allowing you to pause the execution of your app at specific points. There are various types of breakpoints you can use:

- **Standard Breakpoints**: These breakpoints stop the app's execution at a specific line of code. Once the app is paused, you can examine variable values and the current state of your app.

- **Conditional Breakpoints**: These breakpoints pause the app only when a specific condition is met. For example, you may only want to break when a certain variable reaches a particular value.

- **Exception Breakpoints**: These breakpoints are triggered when an exception is thrown in your code. This is useful for catching runtime errors that would otherwise go unnoticed.

- **Symbolic Breakpoints**: These are particularly useful for pausing execution when specific methods or functions are called, even if you don't know exactly where the function is used in the code.

Using the Debugger to Inspect Variables

Once your app is paused at a breakpoint, you can use the Xcode debugger to inspect the values of variables. This can be done in the following ways:

- **Variable Inspector**: This panel shows the current values of all variables in scope. You can expand complex objects to see their properties and even modify values during runtime to observe how changes affect the app's behavior.

- **Print Statements**: Adding `print()` statements to your code allows you to log variable values to the console, providing insight into the app's state as it runs. However, print statements can clutter the output and may not always provide the level of detail needed for complex debugging.

Symbolic Breakpoints and Logging Strategies

Symbolic Breakpoints: Targeting Specific Methods

Symbolic breakpoints are an essential feature for debugging when you want to break execution at a specific method, function, or even a system event, such as a view controller's lifecycle method or network requests. Symbolic breakpoints allow you to target code that may be executed in multiple places without setting a breakpoint on each occurrence. This is especially useful when dealing with third-party frameworks or system functions.

To set a symbolic breakpoint:

1. Open the Breakpoint Navigator in Xcode.

2. Click the "+" button at the bottom-left corner of the navigator and select "Symbolic Breakpoint."

3. Enter the symbol (method or function name) where you want the breakpoint to be triggered. For instance, if you're troubleshooting issues in the

`viewDidLoad` method, you can set a symbolic breakpoint on `-[UIViewController viewDidLoad]`.

Once set, the debugger will pause whenever that function or method is called, regardless of where it is used in your app.

Logging Strategies: Tracking Execution and Understanding Flow

Logging is a crucial strategy for tracking the flow of your app and understanding what's happening at various stages of its execution. While breakpoints allow you to pause the app and inspect its state, logging enables you to monitor the app continuously as it runs, even in production environments.

Here are some best practices for effective logging in Swift:

Use `NSLog()` for Consistency: `NSLog()` is a great way to log messages in a format that includes the timestamp, process ID, and message content. This can be useful for reviewing logs later or for debugging issues that occur intermittently.

NSLog("User tapped on the submit button.")

1.

Create Custom Log Functions: For complex applications, it can be helpful to create custom logging functions that log specific types of information. For instance, you might have a function that logs network requests and responses, or one that logs detailed user interaction events.

```
func logNetworkRequest(_ request: URLRequest) {
    NSLog("Network Request: \(request.url?.absoluteString ?? "unknown URL")")
}
```

2.
3. **Conditional Logging**: In a production environment, verbose logging can negatively impact performance and clutter logs. To mitigate this, consider using a logging framework that supports different log levels (e.g., debug,

info, error) and enables conditional logging based on the environment.

4. **Use Swift's Built-in** `print()`: While `print()` is useful during development, it's less powerful than `NSLog()`, especially in a multi-threaded environment. However, it can still be helpful for quick debugging, especially for smaller apps or when tracking specific values temporarily.

5. **External Logging Services**: For apps running in production, you may want to send logs to an external service like Firebase or Sentry. These services can track errors and exceptions in real-time, helping you respond to issues that occur after deployment.

Crash Tracing and What to Look For

Crashes are inevitable, but how you trace and resolve them can make a significant difference in your app's stability. Swift provides robust tools to help you analyze crash reports and pinpoint the root cause of issues.

Using Crash Reports to Identify Root Causes

Crash reports provide essential information about an app's state when it crashes. The key elements of a crash report typically include:

- **Stack Trace**: The call stack at the time of the crash, which shows the series of method calls leading to the crash. Understanding this can help you identify where in the code the issue occurred.

- **Exception Information**: The type of exception thrown and the specific line of code where it was triggered.

- **Thread Information**: Identifying which thread was executing when the crash occurred can help you understand whether the issue is related to UI updates, background tasks, or concurrency issues.

Xcode integrates with tools like **Xcode Organizer** to allow you to access crash reports for your app. This makes it easier to understand why the app crashed and to track patterns of failure.

Analyzing Memory Leaks and Retain Cycles

Memory management is a common cause of crashes in Swift, especially with reference types and object ownership. Memory leaks or retain cycles can cause apps to crash due to excessive memory usage or failure to release unused objects. The key to preventing these types of issues is to:

- **Use Instruments**: Xcode's Instruments tool can be used to detect memory leaks and retain cycles by tracking object allocations and deallocations.

- **Check for Strong References**: Retain cycles occur when two objects hold strong references to each other, preventing either from being deallocated. Identifying these issues early can prevent crashes related to memory management.

Look for Multi-threading Issues

Crash reports often point to multi-threading issues, such as attempts to update the UI from a background thread or race conditions. To debug such problems, look for:

UI Updates from Background Threads: Swift requires that all UI updates occur on the main thread. Crashes can occur if you try to update the UI from a background thread. Always ensure that UI updates are dispatched on the main queue.

```
DispatchQueue.main.async {
  // Update UI
}
```

-
- **Race Conditions**: These occur when multiple threads access shared data simultaneously without proper synchronization. Use synchronization mechanisms such as locks or serial queues to ensure safe access to shared resources.

Unit Testing and Testable Design in Swift

Unit testing and a testable codebase are essential for reliable software. When tests are clear and concise, they provide confidence that individual components work as intended and that future changes will not introduce regressions. In Swift, leveraging a powerful testing framework alongside a design that anticipates testing needs results in code that is easier to maintain, extend, and verify. This section explores how to write meaningful unit and user interface tests, use mocks and stubs in combination with dependency injection, and employ snapshot testing to guard against unintended visual changes.

Writing Meaningful Unit and UI Tests

A well-constructed test suite verifies behavior, documents intended outcomes, and simplifies refactoring. Both logic-focused unit tests and interaction-driven UI tests play complementary roles in a robust quality process.

Establishing a Strong Foundation for Unit Tests

Unit tests should isolate single units of behavior—typically individual functions or methods. To achieve this:

- **Adopt the Arrange-Act-Assert Pattern**

    1. *Arrange*: Set up inputs and state.

    2. *Act*: Invoke the function under test.

3. *Assert*: Verify that results match expectations.

Name Tests for Clarity

Use descriptive test names that specify the condition under test and the expected result, for example:

func testLoginFailsWhenPasswordIsEmpty() { ... }

-
- **Cover Edge Cases**

  Include tests for boundary conditions, invalid inputs, and error paths. If a function can throw, ensure that error cases are exercised.

- **Limit Test Dependencies**

  Test code should avoid reliance on external systems. Keep tests fast by avoiding network calls or file operations.

- **Use Setup and Teardown for Shared State**

  If multiple tests require common setup, leverage `setUp()` and `tearDown()` to prepare and clean resources, ensuring each test runs in isolation.

Designing Reliable UI Tests

UI tests validate the user journey, confirming that screens appear correctly and interactions produce intended results.

- **Assign Accessibility Identifiers**

  Every interactive element, such as buttons and text fields, should have a unique identifier. This allows tests to locate and manipulate UI components reliably.

- **Structure Tests by Flow**

  Organize UI tests according to user scenarios (e.g., login flow, settings update). Each test should perform a clear sequence of actions and assert final state or visible elements.

- **Manage State Between Runs**
  Ensure a consistent starting point by resetting the application's state before each UI test. This can be done by launching with specific arguments or clearing persisted data.

- **Optimize for Speed and Stability**
  Minimize waits by using expectations that depend on element existence or visibility rather than fixed delays. This reduces flakiness and shortens test execution time.

Mocking, Stubbing, and Dependency Injection

Real-world services, databases, and networks introduce variability that can slow tests and produce non-deterministic results. Mocks and stubs replace these components with controlled implementations, while dependency injection makes substitution straightforward.

Creating and Using Mocks

Mocks are objects that record how they were used, enabling verification that specific methods were called:

Define Protocol-Based Interfaces
For each external dependency, declare a protocol that exposes only the required methods.

```
protocol UserService {
  func fetchProfile(userID: String, completion: @escaping (Result<User, Error>)
-> Void)
}
```

-

Implement a Mock Class

Provide a mock that tracks method invocations and can simulate success or failure:

```swift
class MockUserService: UserService {
  var fetchProfileCalled = false
  var resultToReturn: Result<User, Error>?

  func fetchProfile(userID: String, completion: @escaping (Result<User, Error>)
-> Void) {
    fetchProfileCalled = true
    if let result = resultToReturn {
      completion(result)
    }
  }
}
```

-

Stubbing Data for Predictable Tests

Stubs supply predefined responses without recording interaction details. Use them when the test only needs specific data:

- **Local JSON Files**
  Bundle small JSON fixtures with the test target to simulate API responses.

- **Inline Stubs**
  Provide simple literal data or error values for immediate use in tests.

Leveraging Dependency Injection

Dependency injection ensures that tests can replace real dependencies with mocks or stubs easily:

- **Constructor Injection**
  Pass dependencies into an object's initializer, making it impossible to create the object without providing its collaborators.

- **Property Injection**
  Use when a dependency may be optional or set after initialization.

- **Method Injection**
  Provide dependencies directly to the method under test for fine-grained control.

By designing types to accept interfaces rather than concrete implementations, your production code and test code share the same pathways, reducing discrepancies between test and runtime behavior.

Snapshot Testing for UI Stability

Snapshot testing captures a visual representation of a view and compares it against a reference image on each test run. Any unintended change in layout or styling causes the test to fail, alerting you to regressions before they reach users.

Setting Up Snapshot Tests

- **Choose a Snapshot Framework**
  Integrate a library that supports capturing and comparing images in various environments.

- **Record Reference Images**
  During the first run, save golden images for each view or screen in the test target.

- **Organize by Device and Configuration**
  Store separate snapshots for different screen sizes, orientations, and appearance modes (light/dark).

Writing Snapshot Test Cases

- **Instantiate the View Under Test**

  Create the view or view controller with a fixed frame and deterministic data.

- **Render and Capture**

  Render the view offscreen and produce a PNG or PDF snapshot.

- **Compare to Reference**

  The test library will perform a pixel-by-pixel comparison, highlighting differences if they exceed a defined threshold.

Maintaining Snapshot Suites

- **Review Failures Carefully**

  Confirm that changes are intentional before accepting new reference images.

- **Automate in Continuous Integration**

  Run snapshot tests as part of your build pipeline to catch regressions early.

- **Limit Snapshots to Critical Screens**

  Focus on views where visual consistency is essential, such as branding elements or core user flows.

Performance Optimization That Matters

Improving an application's performance is a continuous process that requires accurate measurement, targeted fixes, and efficient use of diagnostic tools. When executed thoughtfully, performance tuning enhances user experience, conserves device resources, and prolongs battery life. This section covers how to measure key metrics such as memory usage, processor load, and startup time; how to address common bottlenecks in the language; and how to leverage profiling utilities without becoming overwhelmed.

Measuring Memory, Processor Load, and Startup Time

Tracking Memory Consumption

Monitoring an app's memory footprint reveals leaks and excessive allocations. Start by recording memory use during typical user flows—login, data sync, screen transitions—and observe any upward trends that never subside. Key steps include:

- Allocating each model object with care and immediately releasing large buffers when no longer needed.

- Observing the growth of live object counts during navigation. A steadily rising count often signals unbalanced retains or forgotten observers.

- Using light-weight caches for images or data where possible, and capping their total size to prevent runaway growth.

By charting memory usage over time, you can pinpoint screens or operations that introduce significant allocations and focus your efforts there.

Monitoring Processor Load

Excessive CPU consumption drains battery and can lead to thermal throttling. Measure processor use in these ways:

- Record the percent processor time taken by your app during representative tasks—animations, data parsing, or network requests.

- Identify functions that consume disproportionate CPU by sampling them during execution (for example, complex loops or recursive algorithms).

- Compare single-core and multi-core utilization; if a heavy calculation runs entirely on one core, consider dividing work across concurrent units to leverage available cores.

Profiling processor load during idle periods versus active operations helps distinguish between always-on background tasks and spikes tied to specific features.

Assessing Startup Performance

Application launch time has a direct impact on first impressions. To measure startup latency:

- Time from process launch to first visible screen.

- Track the duration of initial setup routines—database migrations, configuration loading, resource prefetching.

- Measure the time until the main event loop begins processing user events.

Minimize launch-time work by deferring noncritical setup—load configuration or large resources after the first screen appears. This yields a snappier start while still completing necessary initialization in the background.

Fixing Performance Bottlenecks in Swift

Identifying Hotspots

Before optimizing, locate the true sources of slowness. Common culprits include:

- Repeated work in drawing routines or layout calculations.

- Blocking tasks on the main execution queue.

- Overuse of reference types leading to frequent memory management operations.

Use short sampling sessions to capture the most expensive call stacks, then review those methods for optimizations.

Optimizing Algorithms and Data Structures

Algorithmic efficiency often yields the biggest gains:

- Replace naïve linear searches on large collections with binary searches or hashed lookups when order isn't essential.

- Use value types for small, frequently created data where copying is cheaper than reference counting overhead.

- Prefer bulk operations (such as mapping or filtering entire arrays) over element-by-element loops when the underlying implementation can batch work.

Refactoring critical loops and data transformations can reduce CPU cycles dramatically, especially in data-intensive applications.

Reducing Memory Footprint

To curb excessive memory allocation:

- Release or reuse temporary buffers rather than allocating new ones on each use.

- Avoid retaining large object graphs in memory; for example, load only visible data in scrolling views and page in additional content as needed.

- Use lazy loading for infrequently used resources, ensuring they occupy space only when required.

Smaller memory footprints reduce paging and improve cache locality, resulting in faster access and lower overall resource use.

Profiling Tools Usage Without Overwhelm

Selecting the Right Profiling Mode

Profiling suites can monitor numerous metrics—time per function, allocation rates, energy impact. To stay focused:

- Run short "time sampling" sessions to find slow methods. This mode records program counters periodically and highlights where your app spends most of its time.

- Switch to allocation tracing only when investigating memory growth, so you avoid the noise of processor data.

- Reserve energy-impact profiles for analyzing background activity, ensuring the app remains efficient when idle.

By concentrating on one metric at a time, you avoid drowning in data and can apply targeted improvements.

Interpreting Profile Results

When reviewing profiles:

- Look for spikes or plateaus in the graph corresponding to user actions. Clicking a button should show a brief CPU burst, not a prolonged peak.

- Examine the list of functions sorted by average time or memory used. Focus first on those that cumulatively consume the most resources.

- Check thread activity to ensure heavy work is off the main execution queue. Main-thread congestion leads to dropped frames and a laggy interface.

Contextualizing each spike with the user action that triggered it makes it easier to connect data to user experience.

Integrating Profiling into Development Workflow

Rather than profiling only at milestones, incorporate it regularly:

- Add lightweight "smoke tests" that exercise key flows and capture basic performance snapshots.

- Automate comparison of memory and CPU metrics over builds to detect regressions early.

- Teach team members how to interpret basic reports, spreading performance awareness throughout the project.

Regular use of profiling tools demystifies performance tuning, turning it from a daunting task into a routine part of development.

App Store-Ready: Build, Sign, and Submit

Releasing an application to end users involves more than simply compiling code. It requires meticulous preparation, correct packaging, and adherence to distribution requirements. This section covers each phase in detail: readying your build, configuring distribution profiles and versioning, and executing a smooth beta and public release.

Preparing your app for release

Removing diagnostic code and optimizing builds

Before creating a release build, strip out any development-only code paths such as verbose logging, debug alerts, or hidden test menus. Ensure that assertions and debug-only frameworks are disabled in your Release configuration. In Xcode, verify that the **Optimization Level** under your Release scheme is set to **Fastest, Smallest [-Os]** (or **Fastest [-O]**, depending on your needs), and disable features like code coverage or address sanitizers. This combination reduces binary size and improves runtime performance.

Validating assets and metadata

Perform an audit of all bundled resources—images, audio, data files—to confirm correct formats and resolutions. Remove unused assets and verify that high-resolution (@2x, @3x) images are provided for every device class you support. Localize static strings and screenshots as needed, and update Info.plist entries such as **CFBundleDisplayName** and **CFBundleShortVersionString** to reflect the final product name and release version. Failing to synchronize metadata across all languages can lead to last-minute rejections.

Finalizing entitlements and permissions

Review the app's entitlements (App Capabilities) section in your project's target settings. Disable any unused services—such as Background Modes, Keychain Sharing, or HealthKit—to minimize surface area for privacy reviews. Confirm that the Usage Description keys (e.g., **NSCameraUsageDescription**, **NSLocationWhenInUseUsageDescription**) contain clear, user-facing explanations for why your app requests sensitive access. Inconsistent or vague permission strings often trigger review delays.

App thinning, provisioning profiles, and versioning

Enabling binary slicing and on-demand resources

App thinning—comprising slicing, bitcode, and on-demand resources—ensures each device downloads only the assets and code it needs. Enable **Bitcode** in your build settings so the distribution platform can re-optimize your binary for future devices. Define on-demand resource tags for large assets that can be fetched dynamically. This approach reduces initial download size and conserves storage on user devices.

Configuring certificates and provisioning profiles

Distribute your app using a Distribution certificate paired with a matching provisioning profile. In the Developer portal, create an **App Store** provisioning profile that binds your app's bundle identifier to your Distribution certificate. Download and install both the certificate and profile in Xcode's **Signing & Capabilities** pane. Ensure that your team's shareable profiles are up to date—expired or mismatched profiles are a leading cause of submission failures.

Applying semantic versioning and build numbering

Adopt a clear versioning scheme: use semantic versioning (MAJOR.MINOR.PATCH) for releases, and increment the build number for each archive you submit. In Info.plist, **CFBundleShortVersionString** holds the public version (for example, 2.1.0), while **CFBundleVersion** holds an internal build identifier (for example, 42). Coordinate these values with your release documentation so testers and users can report issues against precise builds.

Tips for successful TestFlight and public submission

Structuring beta distribution

Use your beta distribution channel to gather feedback and catch critical issues before public launch. In your distribution dashboard, create internal tester groups for rapid iterations and external groups for broader testing. Supply clear install instructions and note known limitations. Encourage testers to report issues with reproducible steps, device model, and operating system version.

Crafting effective release notes and metadata

When inviting testers or users, accompany each build with concise release notes that describe new features, known issues, and testing goals. For the public listing, prepare compelling descriptions and localized screenshots that highlight your app's core value. Provide keywords that accurately reflect user search behavior, and supply high-quality app previews demonstrating key workflows. Omitting any required metadata—such as privacy policy URLs or support contacts—can result in prolonged review times.

Responding to review feedback

Monitor submission status closely and be prepared to respond swiftly to any review questions or rejection reasons. Review teams frequently request demonstrations of in-app purchase flows, user authentication, or location-based features. Provide annotated screenshots or short video clips illustrating these processes. If you need to resubmit, increment the build number and address each concern methodically. Clear communication and prompt updates often expedite approval.

Part V
Professional Practices and Lifelong Maintainability

Code Style, Linting, and Documentation

Establishing a clear and consistent approach to writing Swift code is essential for teams of any size. A well-defined style reduces friction during collaboration, accelerates onboarding of new developers, and ensures that the codebase remains approachable as it grows. Automated linting catches deviations early, while integrated documentation keeps intent and usage front and center. This section outlines best practices for crafting a unified code style, leveraging tools to enforce rules, and setting up conventions that evolve with the team.

Building a Consistent Swift Codebase

A uniform code style minimizes cognitive load when switching between modules or reviewing pull requests. Consistency applies to naming, file layout, formatting, and documentation placement.

Naming and Organization

- **Types and Protocols**
  Use UpperCamelCase for types and protocols. Interfaces that express a capability end in "able" (for example, `Serializable`, `Authenticatable`).

- **Properties and Methods**
  Adopt lowerCamelCase. Method names should read like sentences when combined with their parameter labels, such as `func fetchUserProfile(for userID: String)`.

- **Constants and Enumerations**

  Prefer `let` for constants and group related values in enums. Name enum cases in lowerCamelCase to align with Swift's guidelines.

Organize files by feature rather than by type. For example, a "Profile" folder contains `ProfileViewController.swift`, `ProfileViewModel.swift`, and `ProfileService.swift`. This reduces navigation time and clarifies ownership of code.

Formatting Guidelines

- **Indentation and Spacing**

  Use four spaces per indent level. Avoid tabs to prevent discrepancies in different editors.

- **Line Length**

  Limit lines to 100 characters. Wrap parameters onto multiple lines when necessary, keeping each parameter on its own line for readability.

Braces and Control Flow

Place opening braces on the same line and closing braces on their own line. For control statements, include a space before the parenthesis:

```
if isEnabled {
  performAction()
}
```

-

Document decisions in a central style document. This living guide should describe each rule and explain its rationale, making it easier for newcomers to adopt the standards.

Using SwiftLint and DocC Effectively

Automated tools enforce style rules and generate browsable documentation. Integrating linting and documentation into daily workflows ensures quality without manual overhead.

SwiftLint for Automated Linting

SwiftLint checks your code against a configurable set of rules, flagging style violations and potential bugs.

1. **Installation**

   ○ Homebrew: `brew install swiftlint`

   ○ CocoaPods: add `pod 'SwiftLint'` to your Podfile

   ○ Swift Package Manager: add it as a dependency in your `Package.swift`

Configuration

Create a `.swiftlint.yml` file at the repository root. Enable or disable rules to match your style guide:

```
disabled_rules:
 - force_cast
 - line_length
opt_in_rules:
 - empty_count
line_length:
 warning: 100
 error: 120
```

2.
3. **Custom Rules and Regex**
   When the default rule set is insufficient, define custom patterns to enforce

project-specific conventions, such as naming prefixes or forbidden APIs.

Continuous Integration

Integrate SwiftLint into your CI pipeline to prevent merges when violations occur. A typical step in a script build phase:

```
if brew ls --versions swiftlint >/dev/null; then
  swiftlint lint --strict
fi
```

4.

DocC for Generating Documentation

DocC transforms specially formatted comments into interactive documentation directly in Xcode or as a static website.

Writing Doc Comments

Use triple slashes (/ / /) before declarations. Include parameter and return details:

```
/// Fetches data for the specified user.
///
/// - Parameter userID: The identifier of the user to retrieve.
/// - Returns: A `User` object if found, or `nil` otherwise.
func fetchUser(userID: String) -> User?
```

1.
2. **Organizing Topics**
   Group related symbols into chapters and articles by creating a Documentation Catalog in your project. This structure helps readers navigate concepts and APIs.

3. **Preview and Export**
   In Xcode, select **Help > Build Documentation** to generate and browse locally. For a public site, export the catalog as a static archive and host it on

a web server or via GitHub Pages.

4. **Keeping Docs in Sync**
   As APIs evolve, update documentation comments alongside implementation changes. Treat documentation failures as build errors to ensure completeness.

Team Conventions That Scale

As teams expand, ad hoc conventions fracture into divergent styles. Instituting shared workflows and automations ensures cohesion without micromanagement.

Shared Style Guide and Onboarding

Maintain a `STYLEGUIDE.md` in the repository that consolidates naming rules, formatting standards, lint settings, and documentation practices. New team members can review this single source of truth to ramp up quickly.

Pre-commit Hooks and Automation

Use Git hooks or third-party tools to run linters and formatters before code reaches the remote repository. A sample pre-commit script might run SwiftLint and then `swift-format` to correct minor issues automatically.

```sh
#!/bin/sh
swiftlint lint --fix || exit 1
swift-format format --recursive Sources/ Tests/ || exit 1
```

This prevents style regressions and ensures that every commit adheres to the agreed conventions.

Continuous Review and Evolution

Schedule periodic style audits to remove obsolete rules and refine conventions based on real-world experience. Encourage team feedback via a shared channel or regular meetings to surface pain points and propose improvements.

Document any changes in the style guide and update CI configurations accordingly. By treating style rules as flexible and evolving artifacts, the team can adapt to new language features and changing project needs without sacrificing consistency.

Version Control for Swift Projects

Effective version control is fundamental to maintaining code quality and coordinating development in Swift applications. A well-designed workflow empowers teams to deliver features rapidly, manage releases reliably, and recover from errors with minimal friction. This section examines branching strategies tailored to mobile development, practices for collaborating via distributed version control and continuous integration, and concrete approaches to prevent merge conflicts as the codebase evolves.

Branching strategy for mobile apps

A clear branching model organizes parallel workstreams—features, bug fixes, experiments—while ensuring that production-ready code remains stable. Mobile projects often contend with multiple release tracks, third-party SDK updates, and platform upgrades, making disciplined branch management especially important.

Defining branch roles

- **Mainline**: Serves as the always-deployable base. Every commit here must pass automated checks and review requirements.

- **Development**: Acts as an integration zone for new features. Teams merge feature branches here to verify interaction before promoting to the mainline.

- **Feature branches**: Created per ticket or user story, named to reflect purpose (e.g., `feature/user-authentication`). These isolate work until it's ready for wider testing.

- **Release branches**: Spawned from the development line when preparing a public version. Use this branch to stabilize, finalize notes, and address minor fixes without blocking ongoing feature work.

- **Hotfix branches**: Branched directly from the mainline for urgent corrections in production. After the fix, merge changes back into both the mainline and development branches to keep all lines current.

Naming conventions and lifespan

Consistent branch names enhance clarity:

- Prefix with type: `feature/`, `release/`, `hotfix/`

- Include a concise identifier and reference (such as ticket number)

- Limit lifespan: Delete branches promptly after merge to avoid stale divergence

Short-lived feature branches reduce integration pain by minimizing the volume of changes merged at once.

Synchronizing with upstream changes

Frequent integration is critical. Teams should pull and merge upstream updates into active branches at least daily. This practice:

- Reduces conflict scope

- Exposes integration issues early

- Ensures compatibility with dependency updates such as SDK versions or language toolchain upgrades

Whether merging or rebasing, coordinate with teammates to decide on a consistent approach and avoid rewriting shared history unexpectedly.

Using Git for collaboration and CI integration

A robust collaboration workflow leverages the strengths of distributed version control and integrates automated pipelines that verify quality at every step.

Code review workflows

- **Pull requests**: Contributors submit branches for review, triggering discussions on design, style, and correctness.

- **Review criteria**: Define guidelines for reviewers—test coverage, adherence to style rules, documentation completeness—so feedback is focused and actionable.

- **Approval policies**: Require at least one or two peer approvals before merging, depending on branch criticality. Use status checks to block merges until automated tests pass.

Continuous integration setup

- **Build validation**: On each push to development or feature branches, run a clean build to catch configuration or dependency issues immediately.

- **Automated testing**: Execute unit tests, UI tests, and linting stages. Fail the pipeline on test or style violations to prevent regressions.

- **Artifact generation**: Produce build artifacts—installable bundles or simulator packages—for downstream QA or deployment workflows, ensuring each build is traceable.

Managing access and permissions

- **Role-based permissions**: Grant write access only to trusted integrators for protected branches (mainline, release).

- **Enforce signing rules**: Configure branch protection rules that require successful CI statuses and review approvals before permitting merges.

- **Audit trails**: Rely on the version control system's history to trace who merged what and when, aiding in accountability and post-mortem investigations.

Avoiding merge hell with real workflows

Merge conflicts become more challenging as the team grows and features accumulate. Proactive practices help maintain smooth integration.

Embracing trunk-based development patterns

While longer-lived feature branches have their place, trunk-based approaches encourage developers to commit small, incremental changes directly to the mainline or a short-lived integration branch. This pattern:

- Reduces the window of conflicting edits

- Ensures the mainline always reflects the latest verified state

- Simplifies release preparation, since there is no large consolidation step

Handling conflicts efficiently

When conflicts occur:

- **Narrow the scope**: Pull only the necessary commits for your feature branch before merging.

- **Use interactive rebase**: Clean up local commits, squash trivial changes, and resolve conflicts in a controlled, step-by-step manner.

- **Leverage three-way merges**: Graphical merge tools can visualize difference regions and help preserve intent from both sides.

Document common conflict scenarios and resolution tips in your team handbook to reduce the learning curve for new members.

Maintaining branch hygiene

- **Delete merged branches**: Remove obsolete lines of development to keep the repository clean and reduce clutter in pull request lists.

- **Archive release metadata**: Tag release commits with human-readable version labels (for example, `v1.2.0`) and store release notes in the repository.

- **Schedule periodic pruning**: Remove stale remote branches and obsolete build artifacts to improve repository performance and clarity.

Preparing for the Long Game

Sustaining a codebase over months and years requires deliberate strategies that balance immediate feature work with long-term health. As applications grow, technical debt accumulates, dependencies evolve, and user needs shift. By planning for refactoring, establishing maintenance practices, and architecting for future change, you ensure that your project remains adaptable, stable, and efficient well beyond its initial launch.

Refactoring Legacy Swift Code

Legacy code often reflects decisions made under time pressure or early iterations of the project. Refactoring that code improves readability, reduces hidden bugs, and paves the way for new features.

Assessing Code Health

Begin by profiling areas of highest complexity and most frequent change. Use metrics such as function length, cyclomatic complexity, and code churn to identify hotspots. Review test coverage to uncover untested modules; low coverage often signals fragile code that resists change.

Establishing a Refactoring Plan

1. **Prioritize Critical Paths**
   Target components that directly impact user experience or business logic. Refactor network handling, data transformations, and view-model coordination first, since errors here often have outsized consequences.

2. **Apply Small, Incremental Changes**
   Break the work into scoped tasks—extract a method, rename a class, introduce a protocol. Each change should leave the code compilable and

fully tested.

3. **Leverage Safe Refactoring Tools**

   Modern editors support renaming symbols, extracting methods, and inlining variables with automatic updates. Trust these tools to minimize manual errors.

4. **Integrate Tests Early**

   Where tests are missing, write characterization tests that capture current behavior before refactoring. These tests guard against unintentional regressions as you reorganize code.

Patterns for Migration

- **Introduce Abstractions**

  Define protocols to abstract away concrete implementations. This allows you to replace classes gradually without affecting callers.

- **Modularize by Feature**

  Group related types and logic into discrete modules or packages. Move functionality one feature at a time, updating imports and dependencies as you go.

- **Deprecation and Cleanup**

  Mark outdated methods as deprecated and provide replacements. After client code migrates, remove legacy implementations in a controlled release.

Maintaining Projects Post-Launch

After release, stability and responsiveness to user feedback become paramount. Maintenance encompasses monitoring, updates to third-party libraries, and rapid fixes for emerging issues.

Monitoring and Analytics

Embed lightweight telemetry to track performance metrics and error rates in production. Monitor memory usage, response times, and crash frequency to detect degradation early.

- **Automated Alerts**
  Configure thresholds for key metrics and notify the team when they are exceeded. Early warning gives you time to triage issues before they affect many users.

- **Usage Patterns**
  Analyze feature adoption and navigation flows. Understanding which areas of the app are most active helps prioritize maintenance and optimization work.

Dependency Management

Regularly update external libraries to benefit from bug fixes and security patches. Before upgrading, review changelogs for breaking changes and test thoroughly in a sandbox environment.

- **Lockfile Discipline**
  Use a lockfile to pin dependency versions. This prevents surprise upgrades from destabilizing your build.

- **Staged Rollouts**
  Automate the delivery of updates to a small percentage of users first, observe for issues, then expand the rollout once stability is confirmed.

Issue Response Workflow

Establish a triage process for incoming bug reports:

1. **Categorize Severity**
   Classify issues as critical, major, or minor. Critical bugs warrant immediate

patches; low-priority items can wait for the next feature cycle.

2. **Reproducibility Scripts**

   Create minimal test cases or configuration guides to reproduce issues. This accelerates diagnosis and resolution.

3. **Patch Releases**

   For critical fixes, prepare a hotfix branch, apply the change, run full regression tests, and release promptly. Merge the fix back into the mainline to keep all branches aligned.

Future-Proofing with Modular Design and Testing

Building for tomorrow means architecting code that can evolve without collapse and validating changes continuously.

Embracing Modular Architecture

Divide your application into well-defined modules—UI components, data access, business rules, and utilities. Each module should have a clear public interface and encapsulate its internal details.

- **Loose Coupling**

  Rely on interfaces rather than concrete types. Components communicate through protocols or service abstractions.

- **High Cohesion**

  Keep related functionality together. A module focused on user profiles should contain only code relevant to that domain.

- **Independent Release Cadence**

  Where possible, package modules as separate libraries or packages. This enables you to update one module without rebuilding the entire app.

Building a Robust Test Suite

A comprehensive testing strategy is vital for safeguarding refactoring and modularization efforts.

- **Unit Tests for Logic**
  Cover each module's core behavior with isolated tests. Mock external dependencies to focus each test on its subject.

- **Integration Tests**
  Validate the interaction between modules—data storage with network synchronization, or UI screens with view models.

- **End-to-End Scenarios**
  Automate user workflows to catch issues that slip through lower-level tests. Simulate interactions through the application from start to finish.

- **Continuous Validation**
  Integrate all tests into an automated pipeline. Reject changes that introduce test failures or degrade coverage.

Safeguarding Against Obsolescence

- **Adopt a Plugin-Style Approach**
  Design extension points where new features can be added without altering core modules. For example, register new data sources via a plugin registry.

- **Document Module Contracts**
  Maintain clear interface documentation and versioning guidelines for each module. Specify backward-compatibility guarantees and deprecation policies.

- **Regular Architectural Reviews**
  Every quarter, review the module boundaries and dependency graph. Adjust as necessary to align with evolving requirements and prevent unmanageable

coupling.

Conclusion

The journey through this handbook has presented a structured path for creating applications that are robust, maintainable, and efficient. By grounding your work in solid fundamentals, adopting effective architecture patterns, applying modern language features, and establishing disciplined processes for testing and deployment, you lay the foundation for software that not only meets today's demands but adapts gracefully to tomorrow's challenges.

Recapping Core Principles

Embracing the Language Fundamentals

A mastery of variables, constants, optionals, control flow, closures, enums, and structs forms the bedrock of reliable code. By using immutability where possible, guarding against absent values explicitly, and choosing clear, concise constructs, you reduce the chance of unexpected failures. These basics are not academic exercises—they represent daily tools for expressing logic that is readable, safe, and straightforward to review.

Crafting Sustainable Architecture

From MVC to MVVM and coordinators, selecting the right pattern for each feature ensures separation of concerns and testability. Coordinators keep navigation logic uncluttered, ViewModels encapsulate presentation rules, and protocols define clear contracts. Such separation makes it simpler to refactor, extend, and onboard new collaborators without fear of breaking intertwined code paths.

Integrating Modern Practices

Leveraging Concurrency and Reactive Patterns

Structured concurrency with `async/await` and actors provides a clear model for parallel work that avoids race conditions and deadlocks. Combine's publishers and subscribers add a declarative layer for handling streams of data. When combined with view models, these tools result in user interfaces that remain responsive and resilient, even as complex background tasks unfold.

Optimizing Performance and Reliability

Regular profiling of memory use, processor load, and startup times guides targeted improvements. Instruments help trace leaks and CPU hotspots without overwhelming you, while snapshot testing guards against visual regressions. Together, these techniques maintain the agility of your codebase, ensuring that new features do not degrade existing behavior.

Preparing for Deployment and Future Growth

Streamlining Release Processes

A production-ready build excludes development artifacts, uses optimized compiler settings, and includes only the assets each device requires. Proper versioning and signing with correct profiles, combined with structured beta distribution, accelerate feedback loops and reduce review cycles. A thoughtful approach to release notes, metadata, and tester communication further smooths the path to public availability.

Establishing Maintenance and Evolution

Post-launch work is never "done." By monitoring performance in the field, addressing runtime errors promptly, and updating dependencies in a controlled manner, you keep the application healthy. Modular design and comprehensive testing enable incremental refactoring of legacy code. Regular architectural reviews and deprecation plans prevent technical debt from growing unchecked.

Looking Ahead Beyond This Handbook

Continuous Learning and Community Engagement

Technology advances constantly. New language versions introduce features that reshape best practices, while third-party libraries offer specialized capabilities. Staying active in developer forums, reading official language proposals, and participating in code reviews broadens your perspective and equips you to adopt innovations safely.

Building for Longevity and Adaptability

Ultimately, the most enduring applications combine sound engineering with flexibility. Design extension points that allow new modules to plug in without invasive changes. Document public interfaces and maintain a clear deprecation policy so that consumers of your code can upgrade smoothly. By anticipating change and embedding resilience into your development habits, you create software that remains valuable across years of evolution.

Appendix

This appendix serves as a concise reference to high-value information, tools, and best practices you can use throughout your development process. It gathers definitions, command-line snippets, editor shortcuts, automation examples, and recommended resources so you can quickly locate critical details without hunting through code or documentation.

Glossary of Key Terms

Actor

A protected, concurrent type that isolates its mutable state. Actors serialize access to their properties and methods, preventing data races when multiple concurrent tasks interact with shared data.

Closure

A self-contained block of functionality that can be passed around and executed. Closures capture values from their surrounding context and can be assigned to variables or used as callback handlers.

Protocol

A contract that defines a set of methods, properties, or other requirements. Types conforming to a protocol agree to implement those requirements, enabling polymorphism and dependency inversion.

Generic

A language feature that allows functions, structs, and classes to operate on any type that meets specific constraints. Generics eliminate duplication by enabling code to work with multiple data types in a type-safe way.

Task

A unit of asynchronous work managed by the concurrency system. Tasks can be spawned in structured scopes, cancelled when no longer needed, and can propagate errors via `async`/`await`.

Snapshot Testing

A form of UI testing that captures a rendered view as a reference image. On each test run, the view is rendered again and compared pixel-by-pixel to detect unintended visual changes.

Quick Reference: Swift Fundamentals

Common Keywords and Constructs

- **let** / **var** for immutable and mutable bindings

- **if** / **guard** / **switch** for conditional execution

- **for** / **while** loops for iteration

- **func** to declare functions, including `throws` for error-handling functions and `async` for asynchronous functions

- **enum** for finite state modeling with optional associated values

- **struct** and **class** for value and reference types respectively

Standard Library Types

- **String, Int, Double, Bool** for basic data

- **Array<T>, Dictionary<Key,Value>, Set<T>** for collections

- **Optional<T>** to represent presence or absence of a value

- **Result<Success, Failure>** for encapsulating success or error cases

Error Handling Snippet

```swift
enum DataError: Error { case missing, invalidFormat }
func parse(_ input: String) throws -> Int {
    guard let number = Int(input) else { throw DataError.invalidFormat }
    return number
}
do {
    let value = try parse("42")
    print(value)
} catch {
    print("Parsing failed: \(error)")
}
```

Concurrency Snippet

```swift
actor Counter {
    private var value = 0
    func increment() { value += 1 }
    func get() -> Int { value }
}

Task {
    await Counter().increment()
    let count = await Counter().get()
    print("Count is \(count)")
}
```

Command-Line Cheat Sheet

Building and Testing

Compile and run:

```
swift build
swift run
```

-

Execute tests:

```
swift test
```

-

Package Manager Commands
Create new package:

```
swift package init --type executable
```

-

Add dependency:
In `Package.swift`:

```
.package(url: "https://github.com/owner/repo.git", from: "1.2.3")
```

-

Update packages:

```
swift package update
```

-

Linting and Formatting
Lint project (with SwiftLint installed):

```
swiftlint lint --strict
```

-

Auto-format code (with swift-format configured):

swift-format format --recursive Sources/ Tests/

-

Editor and IDE Shortcuts

While specific key bindings vary by editor, these generic actions are common:

- **Go to definition**: Jump to the declaration of a symbol.

- **Find in files**: Search across the entire workspace for text or symbols.

- **Build and run**: Compile code and launch in the simulator or device.

- **Set breakpoint**: Pause execution on a specific line for inspection.

- **Step over/into**: Advance through code one line or one function call at a time.

- **View call stack**: Inspect the chain of function calls that led to the current point.

Consult your editor's documentation to assign or customize these shortcuts as needed.

Continuous Integration Example

Below is a sample pipeline configuration illustrating automated build, test, and lint stages. Adapt it for your preferred CI system by translating steps into its configuration syntax.

stages:

```
  - lint
  - test
  - build

lint:
  script:
    - swiftlint lint --strict
  allow_failure: false

test:
  script:
    - swift test
  artifacts:
    when: always
    paths:
      - .build/reports/tests/

build:
  script:
    - swift build --configuration release
  artifacts:
    paths:
      - .build/release/
```

Key points:

- **Fail fast** on style or test failures.

- **Store reports** for diagnostics.

- **Produce artifacts** for distribution or manual review.

Recommended Resources

- **Official Language Guide**

  The open-source language reference provides definitive explanations of syntax, types, and standard library APIs.

- **Package Manager Documentation**

  Details on manifest format, dependency resolution, and custom commands.

- **Community Style Guides**

  Publicly maintained guides offer conventions for naming, formatting, and architecture, which can be adapted to your project's needs.

- **Discussion Forums and Issue Trackers**

  Engage with experienced developers to solve challenging problems and keep abreast of emerging patterns.